GEOFFREY ZAKARIAN CAST IRON COOKING
THE DUTCH OVEN

StoreBound

50 Broad Street, New York, NY 10004

ISBN-13: 978-0-9971012-4-9

Printed in China

10987654321

First Edition

Distributed by StoreBound

50 Broad Street, New York, NY 10004

To my mother, Viola, and aunts, Anna, Roxy and Virginia,
Thank you for teaching me the importance of cooking in cast iron.

To my wife, Margaret,
Thank you for pushing me to innovate and think outside the box.

To My Fellow Home Cooks,

This is my first ever cookbook dedicated to Cast Iron Cooking, written to pair perfectly with my Zakarian Non-Stick Cast Iron Dutch Oven. This pan delivers a great punch, just like traditional cast, but even with the most delicate or stickiest ingredients, the clean up is a cinch, I promise.
Here within, you will find my favorite recipes for Dutch oven cooking, utilizing both the base as a traditional Dutch oven and the lid as a skillet pan. Wanting to give you recipes that deliver maximum flavor, I did not hold back. Here, you have access to great cooking techniques and some of my secrets that will deliver big time when the food hits the table.

A few tips to help you through the book:
-Read the recipe through before starting. Planning time appropriately is the most important step.
-Use wooden, plastic or silicone coated tools to preserve and avoid scratches in the coating.
-Order or search about ingredients online if you do not have or they are unfamiliar.
-When a recipe calls for wine, always choose one that you would also be willing to drink.

Thinking back to my youth, I have wonderful memories learning to cook with my aunts and mother in their heritage cast iron. Today, I think of these special women daily and am so proud to use these revolutionary pans with "Zakarian" on them, representing all that they had taught me along the way. How they would have loved and appreciated the ease of these workhorse pans!

I am honored and humbled that you have added this book to your kitchen library and hopeful you too will build family memories around these dishes. Please share pictures of your finished plates - post to social media and tag @geoffreyzakarian and #CastIronChef.

Cheers,

Contents

About the Non-Stick Dutch Oven

Dutch ovens are known as the "do-it-all" of cookware and have been used as cooking vessels for hundreds of years. Originally designed for cooking in a hearth, Dutch ovens are known as casseroles in England and cocottes in France. When it comes to materials, most Dutch ovens are made out of cast iron because they are designed for cooking over long periods of time, whether roasting, braising, frying or baking bread.

The superior non-stick coating on the Zakarian Non-Stick Cast Iron collection is a PFOA & PTFE-free non-stick coating. The coating is stain-resistant, heat safe to 500°F, and non-reactive, meaning it's safe to use with acidic ingredients, like tomatoes. To maintain the longevity of the coating, metal utensils should not be used on the surface. The benefit of non-stick cast iron is the effortless cleanup process. If you've ever cleaned a traditional cast iron pan, you know that it can be a chore and to clean it thoroughly without damaging the seasoning is tricky. With Zakarian non-stick, even sticky foods release cleanly and simply. And unlike traditional uncoated cast iron, you don't have to worry about drying and oiling immediately after use to prevent rust from developing.

The cast-iron itself is the same heavy-duty, durable cast iron that is considered the workhorse of the professional kitchen. Once the pan is pre-heated, its ability to retain heat is unparalleled by stainless steel or aluminum. That makes cast-iron the perfect choice for browning meats, or creating caramelization.

Superior non-stick coating
PFOA & PTFE-free coating
is safe up to 500°F

Double-duty lid
Perfect for gratins, vegetables, crumbles and more, the lid of our oven also functions as a skillet.

6 Quart Capacity
This size Dutch oven is ideal for making stews, roasts, soups, breads and more.

For more Zakarian Non-stick Cast Iron Cookware, check out geoffreyzakarian.com for the full range of products.

MORNING TIME

Shirred Eggs with Griddled Sourdough | 11

Dutch Baby Pancake with Strawberry Jam | 13

Perfect Porridge | 15

Overnight Cinnamon Rolls with Cream Cheese Icing | 17

Huevos Rancheros with Refried Beans and Salsa Verde | 19

Broccoli Rabe & Sausage Frittata | 20

Crispy Hashbrown Skillet Potatoes with Chives and Sour Cream | 21

* Broccoli Rabe and Sausage Frittata on page 20
* Crispy Hashbrown Skillet Potatoes with Chives and Sour Cream on page 21

9

Shirred Eggs with Griddled Sourdough

SERVES : 4   PAN USED : Base & Lid

INGREDIENTS :

2 tablespoons unsalted butter, melted

8 large eggs

8 tablespoons heavy cream

¼ cup Parmesan cheese, shredded

2 tablespoons fresh chives, minced

Kosher salt and freshly ground pepper

4 thick slices sourdough bread

Salted butter for griddling

PREPARATION :

1. Generously brush 4 ovenproof ramekins with melted butter. Crack two eggs into each ramekin; top evenly with cream, Parmesan, chives, Kosher salt and freshly ground pepper.

2. Place ramekins into Dutch oven. Fill with water about an inch up the sides of the ramekin. Carefully transfer Dutch oven. Bake for 12 to 15 minutes in 350°F oven or until egg whites are just set and yolks are still slightly runny (or cook to desired doneness).

3. While eggs are cooking, generously butter both sides of bread. Heat lid of Dutch oven over medium heat. Working in two batches, toast both sides of bread until golden brown. Cut in half and serve with shirred eggs.

Pro Tip :

Shirred, or baked eggs, are a blank canvas. Add vegetables from your dinner last night or crumble some crispy bacon on top. You can also bake a larger portion of eggs for a crowd in the top pan of the Dutch oven by cracking the eggs directly into a buttered pan. Just adjust your bake time accordingly.

Dutch Baby Pancake with Strawberry Jam

SERVES : 4 - 6   PAN USED : Lid

INGREDIENTS :

Jam:

2 pounds fresh strawberries

4 cups sugar

¼ cup lemon juice

Dutch baby:

3 large eggs

1½ tablespoons granulated sugar

¼ teaspoon Kosher salt

¾ cup whole milk, warm

1 teaspoon vanilla extract

¾ cup all-purpose flour

3 tablespoons of unsalted butter, divided

Fresh strawberries, sliced

1 cup of heavy cream, whipped to soft peaks

PREPARATION :

To make the jam:

1. In a wide bowl, crush strawberries in batches until you have 4 cups of mashed berry. In a heavy bottomed saucepan, mix together the strawberries, sugar, and lemon juice. Stir over low heat until the sugar is dissolved. Increase heat to high, and bring the mixture to a full rolling boil. Boil, stirring often, until the mixture reaches 220°F.

To make the Dutch baby:

1. Preheat the oven to 400°F. Melt 1 tablespoon of butter in microwave or small pan. Combine the eggs, granulated sugar, salt, milk, vanilla, flour and melted butter in a blender or food processor and blend until smooth.

2. Preheat lid by placing in oven for 10 minutes. Take out of oven and place 2 tablespoons of butter in top and swirl until melted. Pour the batter into the heated skillet and then immediately, and carefully, move the skillet back to the oven and bake for 25-30 minutes. The pancake is done when it is a rich amber color and the sides have risen considerably. Carefully remove the pan from the oven and let cool slightly on a wire rack.

3. Cut into wedges and serve Dutch baby with a spoonful of warm jam, freshly sliced strawberries, and a mountain of freshly whipped cream.

Pro Tip :

Craving something savory instead of sweet? Leave out the vanilla in the batter, and toss in some freshly snipped herbs. Once baked, top with your favorite savory breakfast options such as avocado, fried eggs, shaved ham or smoked salmon and season with Kosher salt and freshly ground pepper.

Perfect Porridge

SERVES : 4   PAN USED : Base & Lid

INGREDIENTS :

3 cups whole milk, or more, to taste

Zest of ½ orange, removed with a vegetable peeler

3 tablespoons maple syrup

¼ teaspoon ground cinnamon, plus more for sprinkling

Pinch of Kosher salt

1 cup steel-cut oats

½ cup dried medjool dates, chopped

¼ cup pecans, toasted and chopped

1 banana, sliced

PREPARATION :

1. In the lid of the Dutch oven, combine the milk, orange zest, maple syrup, cinnamon and salt. Bring to a simmer.

2. Put the oats into the Dutch oven and ladle in half the warm milk mixture. Bring to a simmer and cook until absorbed, about 8 minutes. Add the rest of the milk a ladle at a time, waiting for it to be absorbed before moving on (as if you were making risotto). The entire process will take 20 to 25 minutes, depending on the brand of oats you buy, ending up with a thick creamy porridge. If you want a slightly soupier porridge, stir in another ¼ cup or so of milk at the end. Discard the orange zest and serve the porridge warmed in bowls. Top each serving with some of the dried dates, toasted pecans, and sliced bananas. Don't forget to sprinkle with extra cinnamon!

Pro Tip :

To make a coconut flavored porridge, reduce the amount of whole milk to 1 ½ cups and combine with one 14 ounce can of coconut milk. Proceed with the rest of the recipe as directed. Top with some unsweetened toasted coconut, chia seeds, and fresh mango chunks.

Overnight Cinnamon Rolls with Cream Cheese Icing

SERVES : 10   PAN USED : Lid

INGREDIENTS :

Dough:

½ cup unsalted butter, melted

½ cup granulated sugar

1 teaspoon Kosher salt

2 eggs

4 cups all-purpose flour

2 packages RAPID RISE yeast

1 cup whole milk, warm

Filling:

½ cup granulated sugar

½ cup light brown sugar

1½ tablespoons ground cinnamon

½ cup unsalted butter, softened

Icing:

4 ounces cream cheese, softened

4 tablespoon unsalted butter, softened

1 teaspoon vanilla extract

2-3 tablespoons milk

2 cups powdered sugar

¼ teaspoon Kosher salt

PREPARATION :

1. Mix butter, sugar and salt in a large bowl. Add eggs. Add in flour and yeast. Stir to combine. Add in milk and mix well until soft, smooth dough forms. Turn out on lightly floured surface. Knead a few times then place into a large bowl that has been well oiled. Alternatively you could use a stand mixer fitted with a dough hook. Cover and let dough rise in a draft free location for at least 30 minutes or until almost doubled in size.

2. Meanwhile, combine sugar, brown sugar and cinnamon in a small bowl. Once the dough has risen, punch down and dump onto well floured work area. Roll into a 14 x 8-inch rectangle on a lightly floured surface. Brush evenly with softened butter and sprinkle filling over buttered dough. Roll up from long side and pinch closed at seam. Cut into 10 cinnamon rolls.

3. Place cinnamon rolls in top pan of Dutch oven that has been brushed with butter. At this point you can cover the rolls with plastic wrap and place rolls in the fridge to bake the following morning.

4. The next morning, remove rolls from fridge 60 minutes prior to the time you will start baking them and leave to rest in a warm spot in your kitchen. Meanwhile, make icing. In mixing bowl with paddle, cream together softened cream cheese and softened butter. Add in vanilla, salt and milk and mix until well combined. Add in powdered sugar and mix until smooth and creamy. If you would like your frosting thicker, add more powdered sugar, one tablespoon at a time and mix well. If you would like a thinner frosting, add more milk, one teaspoon at a time and mix well, until desired consistency is reached.

5. Preheat oven to 350°F. Once oven is heated, bake rolls for approximately 20-25 minutes, or until golden brown and baked through. Let cool for 15 minutes then ice generously with cream cheese icing.

Pro Tip :

Use unflavored dental floss to prevent squishing your rolls while cutting. Slide it under the roll, then bring it up, cross it at the top and pull both ends to cut through roll easily, repeating for each roll.

Huevos Rancheros with Refried Beans & Salsa Verde

SERVES : 6   PAN USED : Base & Lid

INGREDIENTS :

Ranchero sauce:

1 tablespoon olive oil

2 shallots, peeled and chopped

2 cloves garlic, minced

15 ounces tomato sauce

12 ounces roasted piquillo peppers
or roasted red peppers

4.5 ounces green chiles

1 cup chicken stock

1 tablespoon ground cumin

1 tablespoon brown sugar

½ cup heavy cream

Black beans:

4 tablespoons extra virgin olive oil

1 cup onion, thinly sliced

1 jalapeno, seeded and thinly sliced

3 garlic cloves, chopped

2 15-ounce can black beans, drained and rinsed

¼ cup fresh lime juice

Green tabasco sauce

Kosher salt and freshly ground pepper, to taste

Assembly:

Canola oil, for frying the tortillas

6 corn tortillas

Kosher salt

6 large eggs

4 ounces crumbled queso fresco

½ cup fresh cilantro, chopped

Lime wedges, for serving

1 avocado, sliced

PREPARATION :

1. First, prepare the Ranchero sauce. Place Dutch oven over medium heat and add the oil and shallots. Saute the shallots for 2 minutes, then add the garlic and saute another 1-2 minutes. Add all remaining ingredients, except for the heavy cream. Simmer the ranchero sauce for 10 minutes. Remove from heat. Using an immersion blender or regular blender, puree the ranchero sauce until smooth. Then stir in the heavy cream. Salt to taste. Set aside.

2. To prepare the black beans, heat top pan of Dutch oven over medium heat. Add the oil. When the oil is hot, add the onion and jalapeno and cook until the onion is softened, about 8 minutes. Add the garlic, beans, and stock. Bring to a simmer and cook until the liquid is reduced by half, about 15 minutes, mashing the beans a little with the back of a wooden spoon to thicken the sauce. Stir in the lemon juice and Tabasco and salt to taste. Keep warm, stirring in the cilantro just before serving. Remove beans to a bowl and set aside.

3. When ready to serve, heat 2 tablespoons of oil in the lid of Dutch oven and add the tortillas, turning once until light golden on each side. Add black beans in an even layer, followed by dollops of the ranchero sauce, almost covering the beans. Make 5 wells in the beans and sauce and crack a whole egg into each hole.

4. Bake for 20-25 minutes or until whites are set and yolks are still runny. Top with crumbled queso fresco and cilantro. Spoon onto plates and serve with avocado slices and lime wedges.

Pro Tip :

Huevos rancheros are a fun way to mix up the traditional eggs for breakfast (and are also an inexpensive family dinner!). Even though there are a lot of components, the bean sauce and rancheros sauce can be made the day before and rewarmed.

Broccoli Rabe and Sausage Frittata

SERVES : 8   PAN USED : Base & Lid

INGREDIENTS :

1 pound broccoli rabe, tough stem ends removed

¾ pound hot Italian sausage, loose or in links

2 tablespoons extra-virgin olive oil

1 medium onion, diced

Salt and black pepper

1 clove garlic, minced

1 tablespoon basil, roughly chopped

1 ball of burrata, torn into rough pieces

¾ cup Parmesan, grated

10 eggs, lightly beaten

Kosher salt and freshly ground pepper, to season

PREPARATION :

1. Heat oven to 350°F. Bring a large quantity of salted water to a boil in your Dutch oven. Add broccoli rabe and blanch for one minute. Drain and rinse with cold water. Roughly chop greens, press out excess water, and set aside.

2. Heat lid of Dutch oven over medium-high heat. Add sausage (remove casings from links first) and cook, until you have well-browned pieces, 6 to 8 minutes. Remove cooked sausage onto paper towels, and set aside.

3. Add olive oil to skillet. When oil is hot, add onion and cook until softened, about 5 minutes. Season well with Kosher salt and freshly ground pepper, then add garlic and cook for 1 minute more. Turn off heat and stir in chopped greens and reserved sausage. Let mixture cool in pan.

4. Break up ball of burrata and scatter over greens mixture, then sprinkle evenly with Parmesan and basil. Pour seasoned eggs over, tilting pan to distribute.

5. Bake for 30 to 35 minutes, until top is golden and eggs are set in the center. Let cool for 10 minutes, then cut into wedges and serve.

Pro Tip :

Frittata makes an excellent light lunch served with a simple mesclun salad. You could always swap in other toppings and cheeses to customize to your family's tastes and preferences. Use whatever is freshest and in season or as a great dish to help clean out the fridge!

* Photo on page 9

Crispy Hash Brown Skillet Potatoes with Chives and Sour Cream

SERVES : 6 - 8   PAN USED : Lid

INGREDIENTS :

5 russet potatoes, peeled (about 3 pounds)

1½ teaspoons Kosher salt

¼ teaspoon freshly ground black pepper

8 tablespoons vegetable oil, divided

¼ cup chives, minced

Coarse sea salt

PREPARATION :

1. On large hole of box grater, or a food processor, shred potatoes. Place in a colander and rinse well with cold water. Let drain, then wring out excess water in a towel. Place dry potatoes in a large bowl and season with Kosher salt and freshly ground pepper, tossing to coat.

2. Heat lid of Dutch oven over medium heat. Add 4 tablespoons of oil and swirl to coat. Add half of the potatoes in a single layer and press down evenly. Sprinkle with half of the chives. Add the remaining potatoes into the pan spreading evenly. Press down firmly. Cook until golden brown on bottom. Place an oval plate over top of pan and flip hashbrown onto plate. Add remaining oil, and slide potatoes back into pan. Cook until underside is also golden brown and cooked through.

3. Remove from heat and let cool for 5 minutes. Cut into wedges and serve with sour cream and a sprinkle of chives.

Pro Tip :

In Switzerland, this dish is called a Rosti. Recipe ingredients vary to include bacon, rosemary, caraway seeds, eggs, pasta, cheese, even coffee. Serve it for breakfast along side eggs, or for dinner with pork chops and applesauce.

Photo on page 9

SOUPS AND STEWS

Classic Chicken Noodle Soup with Root Vegetables | 24

Black Bean Soup with Spicy Chorizo | 25

Creamy Broccoli Soup with Lemon and Ricotta | 28

Red Lentil and Sweet Pepper Soup | 29

Cream of Asparagus Soup with Kale | 31

New England Clam Chowder | 33

Chilled Corn Soup with Crab | 35

Mushroom Barley Bisque | 37

Game Time Turkey Chili with Avocado Crema | 39

Moroccan Chickpea Stew | 41

Shrimp Gumbo | 43

Classic Chicken Noodle Soup with Root Vegetables

SERVES : 6 - 8   PAN USED : Base

INGREDIENTS :

1 chicken, trimmed of excess fat (about 4 pounds)

3 quarts chicken stock

1 cup carrot, diced

1 cup parsnip, diced

1 cup celery, diced

1 cup leek, well rinsed, thinly sliced (white and light green parts)

Fresh dill, snipped for garnish (optional)

¼ cup white wine

5 sprigs fresh thyme

3 dried bay leaves

½ teaspoon dried oregano

Kosher salt

Cooked egg noodles

PREPARATION :

1. Rinse the chicken well and put in the base of the Dutch oven, so there is 1 or 2 inches of space between the chicken and the walls of the pot. Add chicken stock to cover, about 3 quarts, more if needed. Bring to a boil and then, gently simmer until the chicken is tender throughout, about 60 to 75 minutes, skimming and discarding the foam from the top as you go. Remove the chicken to a bowl and let cool. Pull the chicken meat from the carcass, discarding the skin. Chop or shred the chicken meat into bite - sized pieces.

2. Skim any foam and fat from the top of the chicken broth and discard. Return the stock to a simmer. Add the carrots, celery, leeks, wine, thyme, bay leaves, and oregano. Season with salt. Simmer until the vegetables are tender, about 20 minutes.

3. Add the reserved chicken meat and stir to distribute heat. Put about ½ cup cooked egg noodles in bottom of your bowl. Ladle hot soup over and sprinkle with fresh dill, if desired.

Pro Tip :

If you want to make a truly exceptional chicken soup, order an air chilled Kosher bird from your butcher. It will yield a delicious chicken broth.

Photo on page 26

Black Bean Soup with Spicy Chorizo

SERVES : 6 - 8   PAN USED : Base & Lid

INGREDIENTS :

1 pound black beans, dried

6 ounces chorizo

1 tablespoon extra virgin olive oil

1½ cups sweet onions, such as Vidalia, sliced (1 medium onion)

3 cloves garlic, minced

1 cup carrots, roughly chopped (2 medium carrots)

1 cup celery, roughly chopped (2 medium stalks)

2 tablespoons smoked paprika

1 teaspoon freshly ground black pepper

1 tablespoon Kosher salt

1 large smoked ham hock (2 to 3 pounds)

2 teaspoons dried crumbled sage

2 teaspoons dried marjoram

1 fresh bay leaf

½ cup sour cream

⅓ cup dry white wine or fino sherry

12 piquillo peppers, canned

¼ cup flat leaf parsley, finely chopped

PREPARATION :

1. Preheat the oven to 350°F. Place the beans in the base of the Dutch oven with enough water to cover by several inches, about 6 cups. Bring the water to a boil over medium heat, then reduce the heat and simmer the beans until slightly soft, about 15 minutes. Skim off any foam that rises to the surface. Drain the beans and reserve.

2. Meanwhile, cut the chorizo into ¼ inch cubes. Place the olive oil in your Dutch oven base over medium heat. Add the ham and cook for about 5 minutes, rendering as much fat as possible. Add the onions and sweat, stirring occasionally, until they are translucent, about 15 minutes. Add the garlic, carrots, and celery, and cook, stirring frequently, until the garlic is tender and the rest of the vegetables begin to soften slightly more. Stir in the paprika and black pepper, cook for 1 minute, then add 2 ½ quarts (10 cups) of cold water. Raise the heat to high and bring the liquid to a boil. Add the reserved beans, salt to taste, the ham hock, sage, marjoram, and bay leaf.

3. Cover the pot with the Dutch oven lid and place it in the preheated oven (or simmer slowly on the stovetop) until the beans are very soft, the ham hock is pulling away from the bone, and the liquid is reduced by almost one third, about 4 hours.

4. Remove the ham hock, and reserve; remove the bay leaf. Puree the soup with an immersion blender or in a regular blender. (If it is too thick, thin it with a little water). Season to taste with additional Kosher salt and freshly ground pepper. Reheat the soup over medium flame. Dice the ham hock to use as a garnish. Finish the soup with sour cream and dry white wine. Ladle hot into bowls, garnish with diced piquillo peppers and diced ham hock.

Pro Tip :

Hazelnuts are a great complimentary flavor to this soup. Garnish with toasted hazelnuts and a drizzle of hazelnut oil for an elevated weeknight dinner.

* Photo on page 26

01

02

03

04

Creamy Broccoli Soup with Lemon and Ricotta

SERVES : 6 - 8   PAN USED : Base & Lid

INGREDIENTS :

3 white leeks, cut in half lengthwise, rinsed and thinly sliced

1 stick butter, unsalted

6 medium sized heads of broccoli

¾ cup heavy cream

6 slices of bacon, cut into matchsticks

3 quarts chicken stock

1 cup Italian parsley, chopped

2 lemons, juiced and zested

1 cup of whole milk ricotta, for garnish

½ cup pine nuts, toasted

2 tablespoons dill, chopped

PREPARATION :

1. Sweat the leeks in the base of your Dutch oven with the butter and a pinch of salt until they become tender and translucent. While the leeks are sweating, shave the florets off the top of broccoli and finely dice the rest (keep separate). Once the leeks are soft and tender add in the chicken stock and bring to a rapid boil. Add the finely diced broccoli (not florets) and cook for 3 to 5 minutes, until tender. Add the parsley and puree immediately in a blender. Cool in an iced bath, add cream and season to taste.

2. Cook the bacon in the top of your Dutch oven until the fat has rendered out and they are crispy. Strain on paper towels and reserve the bacon at room temperature. Pour out all but 1 tablespoon of bacon grease and quickly saute the florets in the grease until bright green, season to taste.

3. Place the florets in the center of the bowl and ladle in the soup. Sprinkle the bacon lardons around and add a squirt of lemon juice. Garnish with a dollop of fresh ricotta, dill and toasted pine nuts.

Pro Tip :

Cutting bacon into matchsticks and frying make a great garnish for a frisee salad with poached egg, quiche, baked potatoes, or even a pizza

Photo on page 27

Red Lentil and Sweet Pepper Soup

SERVES : 8 - 10   PAN USED : Base & Lid

INGREDIENTS :

2-16 ounce boxes of red lentils

2 medium carrot, peeled and cut into large pieces

2 medium white onion, peeled and quartered

4 celery stalks, cut into large pieces

2 red bell peppers, diced

4 slices of smoked bacon, cut into ¼ inch pieces

6 slices of pancetta, julienned

3 quarts flavorful chicken stock or vegetable stock

4 sprigs of thyme

2 fresh bay leaf

1 head of garlic, cut in half-crosswise

½ cup dry white wine (or substitute 100ml dry white wine and 50ml dry sherry)

¼ cup heavy cream

2 tablespoons chardonnay vinegar

Kosher salt and freshly ground pepper, to taste

PREPARATION :

1. In the base of your Dutch oven, sweat smoked bacon, onion, carrots, garlic, bay leaf, thyme, celery, and red peppers until the vegetables are very soft. Add in the lentils, cook for a few minutes. Then, add the stock to cover the lentils, bring to simmer and cook very gently until lentils are very soft, about 20-30 minutes. With a skimmer or slotted spoon, remove some of the lentils and set aside.

2. After the lentils are cooked and very tender, transfer them to a food processor or blender, puree until very smooth. (Option: Once pureed, pass through a fine strainer.) Return this puree to a clean saucepot and bring to boil, add in the heavy cream, dry white wine, the chardonnay vinegar and Kosher salt and freshly ground pepper to taste. Thin with a little more stock if necessary. Keep warm.

3. In lid of Dutch oven, over high heat, sauté the julienned pancetta until crisp. Add in the cooked lentils (that were reserved). Season to taste. Garnish bowls of soup with the bacon and lentil mixture.

Pro Tip :

Lentils are low in calories, rich in iron and folate and an excellent source of protein. Change up the flavor profiles in this soup by substituting the cream with coconut milk and adding a tablespoon of red curry paste.

Photo on page 27

Cream of Asparagus Soup with Kale

SERVES : 6 - 8   PAN USED : Base & Lid

INGREDIENTS :

1 pound tender, young kale, stems and ribs removed, coarsely chopped

Kosher salt and fresh pepper to taste

4 tablespoons extra virgin olive oil, divided

1 small onion, chopped

1 medium leek, thoroughly cleaned and chopped (white part only)

1 stalk celery, chopped

1 small parsnip, peeled and chopped

4 bunches of asparagus (about 3 pounds)

2 cups chicken stock, low sodium

1 cup cilantro leaves

1 cup flat leaf parsley

1 13 oz can full fat coconut milk

PREPARATION :

1. Place the kale in the lid of the Dutch oven. Add Kosher salt and freshly ground pepper and about 2 tablespoons olive oil. Stir until kale wilts, about 5 minutes. Transfer the kale to a bowl and reserve.

2. Place the other 2 tablespoons of oil in the base of the Dutch oven over medium low heat. Add the onion, leek, celery, and parsnips and sweat, stirring occasionally, until the vegetables are tender, about 20 minutes. Chop the asparagus stalks, discarding the tough bottom ends. Add the chopped asparagus stalks to the pot and cook until tender, about 15 minutes. Add 2 cups of water and the stock and bring to a simmer.

3. Season the soup with Kosher salt and freshly ground pepper, and simmer over medium low heat another 15 minutes.

4. Allow the soup to cool for easier handling, then puree it in a blender in two batches, adding half the kale, cilantro and parsley to each batch. Add can of coconut milk and stir. Return to Dutch oven and gently reheat over medium low heat until hot.

Pro Tip :

Any leafy green can be used in this soup in place of the kale. Not a fan of kale? Substitute equal amounts of spinach.

New England Clam Chowder

SERVES : 8   PAN USED : Base & Lid

INGREDIENTS :

2 cans clam, drained and chopped, juice reserved

6 tablespoons extra-virgin olive oil

6 slices bacon, chopped (about ½ cup)

2 cups onion, chopped

2 cups celery, chopped

4 tablespoon fresh thyme, chopped

½ cup all-purpose flour

2 quarts chicken stock

4 medium russet potatoes, peeled and diced, (about 2 pounds)

3 cups fresh shucked clams, chopped

1½ cups heavy cream

Kosher salt and freshly ground black pepper

4 tablespoons fresh parsley, chopped

Lemon wedges, for serving

Oyster crackers, for serving

PREPARATION :

1. Heat the base of your Dutch oven over medium heat. Add 1 tablespoon of olive oil and bacon, cooking until crisp, about 4 minutes. Drain on paper towels and discard the bacon fat.

2. Add the remaining 2 tablespoons oil to the pot. Add the onion, celery, and thyme. Cook, stirring occasionally, until the onion is softened, about 8 minutes. Sprinkle the flour over the vegetables and stir to coat the vegetables. Cook until the flour smells toasty, but not browned, about 3 minutes. Pour in the stock, clam juice, and 1 cup water , then bring to a simmer and add the potatoes. Simmer until the potatoes are tender, about 15 minutes.

3. Add the fresh clams and cream and return to a simmer. Cook until the clams are tender, about 5 minutes more. Stir in canned clams. Season with Kosher salt and freshly ground pepper and stir in canned clams. Remove the bay leaves. Serve with lemon wedges and oyster crackers.

Pro Tip :

While it may be more common to use water or fish stock to make this type of soup, I prefer using chicken stock, as it has a level of gelatin from the bones of the chicken used to make it. Although a small amount, it really pulls the soup together. To amp up the soup, smoke your chopped canned clams before adding in to the soup by spreading in a single layer in the lid of the Dutch oven and placing in a covered grill set to 180°F for 30 minutes.

Chilled Corn Soup with Crab

SERVES : 6 - 8   PAN USED : Base & Lid

INGREDIENTS :

6 ears fresh corn, husked

4 tablespoons unsalted butter

2 medium sweet onion, such as Vidalia, chopped

1 small shallot

2 cups heavy cream

1 teaspoon freshly grated nutmeg

8 ounces fresh lump crabmeat, picked over for shells

2 tablespoons chives, finely sliced

2 tablespoons freshly squeezed lemon juice

PREPARATION :

1. Cut the kernels off the corn cobs and reserve them. Place the cobs in the Dutch oven base with 6 cups of water. Bring the water to a boil over high heat, then reduce the heat and simmer for 30 minutes. Pass corn broth through a strainer and reserve.

2. Place the butter in the lid of the Dutch oven over medium heat; add the onion and shallot and cook, stirring occasionally, until the shallot is tender but not yet beginning to brown, about 10 minutes. Add the corn kernels, stir for 1 to 2 minutes, then add the corn broth. Gently simmer until the corn is tender about 30 minutes; the time will vary widely depending upon the age and variety of the corn.

3. Using a slotted spoon, transfer the vegetables to a blender. Add about 1 ½ cups of the cooking liquid (reserve any remaining liquid to thin the soup if necessary). Puree the corn with the broth for 5 minutes. Stir in the cream. Press the mixture through a fine strainer, thinning if necessary with reserved corn broth or water. Stir in the nutmeg, then season with Kosher salt and freshly ground pepper to taste. Allow the soup to cool to room temperature, then chill in the refrigerator.

4. Place the cold soup in chilled cups. Garnish with the lump crab meat, a sprinkle of chives, and a squeeze of lemon juice.

Pro Tip :

Stockpile corn cobs in freezer bags along with other vegetable scraps to add a golden hue and summery sweetness to your vegetable broth.

Mushroom Barley Bisque

SERVES : 6 - 8   PAN USED : Base & Lid

INGREDIENTS :

3 tablespoons extra virgin olive oil

1½ pounds mixed mushrooms, portabella, cremini, shiitake and button, thinly sliced

6 ounces pancetta, cut into ½ inch cubes

2 medium carrot, chopped (about 1 cup)

2 celery stalks, chopped (about ½ cup)

1/2 cup leek, well rinsed, thinly sliced (white and light green parts)

1 medium onion, chopped (about 1 cup)

4 large garlic cloves, finely chopped

2 sprigs fresh Italian parsley

2 sprigs fresh rosemary

2 sprigs fresh thyme

2 dried bay leaves

2 cups dry white wine

1 28-ounce can San Marzano tomatoes with juice, crushed by hand

3 cups chicken stock

½ teaspoon ground allspice

Kosher salt and freshly ground pepper

½ cup pearl barley

1 tablespoon unsalted butter

1 cup crustless day old bread, diced into small cubes

2 tablespoons fresh Italian parsley, chopped

Cheese cloth

Butcher string

PREPARATION :

1. Heat the base of your Dutch oven over medium-high heat. Add the oil. When the oil is hot, brown the mushrooms in batches in a single layer, removing to a plate as the pieces are browned. (Don't salt the mushrooms yet, as you won't obtain a proper sear.)

2. When all the mushrooms are removed, add the pancetta and cook just to render the fat, about 4 minutes. Add the carrot, celery, leek, onion, and half the garlic. Sweat over medium heat until the onion and leek are tender, about 10 minutes.

3. Meanwhile place parsley, rosemary, thyme, lemon and orange zest, cinnamon sticks and bay leaves on top of a piece of cheese cloth, gather edges, and tie closed with string making a purse. Once the vegetables are sweated, pour in the wine and raise the heat to high to reduce the wine by half. Add the sachet, the tomatoes, stock, and allspice. Bring to a simmer and season with Kosher salt and freshly ground pepper. Return the mushrooms to the pot, cover, and simmer until the the broth has thickened but the sauce is still soupy, about 1 hour.

4. Meanwhile, cook the barley in plenty of salted water until tender but still chewy, about 30 to 40 minutes. Drain well.

5. In a small skillet, melt the butter over low heat. Add the bread cubes and cook, tossing, until crisp and browned, about 8 to 10 minutes. In a small bowl, stir together the remaining garlic and the chopped parsley.

6. When the mushrooms are tender and the broth has thickened, add the cooked barley and simmer to blend the flavors, about 15 minutes. Discard the sachet. To serve, ladle into bowls and top each serving with some of the garlic/-parsley mixture and croutons.

Pro Tip :

When sauteing or roasting any vegetable, leave plenty of room for browning. Crowding the pan will create steam and prevent caramelization.

38

Game Time Turkey Chili with Avocado Crema

SERVES : 8 - 10   PAN USED : Base

INGREDIENTS :

3 tablespoons extra virgin olive oil

3 pounds ground turkey, light and dark meat

Kosher salt and freshly ground pepper

2 large onions, chopped (about 3 cups)

6 garlic cloves, finely chopped

2 bunches scallions (white and green parts), chopped (about 2 cups)

2 tablespoons tomato paste

4 tablespoons chili powder

1 12-ounce bottle dark beer, such as Dos Equis

2-28 oz cans fire roasted tomatoes with juice, crushed by hand

1-15.5 ounce can small white beans, drained and rinsed

2 cups chicken stock

2 tablespoons green Tabasco

1 cup full fat yogurt

1 ripe avocado, crushed until smooth

PREPARATION :

1. In the base of your Dutch oven, heat the oil over, medium-high heat. When the oil is hot, add the turkey. Cook and stir occasionally until the turkey is browned all over and you can hear a slight crackling in the pot signaling the moisture has cooked away, about 15 minutes. Season with Kosher salt and freshly ground pepper.

2. Reduce the heat to medium. Add the onions, garlic, and scallions and cook until wilted, about 5 minutes. Make a space in the pan and drop in the tomato paste. Let toast for 1 minute and then stir into the turkey. Sprinkle in the chili powder. Cook and stir until fragrant, about 2 minutes.

3. Pour in the beer and cook, until almost reduced away, about 4 minutes. Pour in the tomatoes, white beans and stock and season with the green Tabasco. Adjust the heat so the chili is gently simmering and cook, uncovered, until the chili is thick and flavorful, about 1 ½ hours.

4. While the chili is simmering, make the avocado crema. Combine crushed avocado and yogurt and whisk until smooth. Chill until needed.

5. Serve chili in bowls with a dollop of avocado crema and garnishes.

Pro Tip :

Have fun with your garnishes! Chili is perfect for a crowd. Set out large bowls of sharp shredded cheddar, lime slices, chopped cilantro and broken tortilla chips.

Moroccan Chickpea Stew

SERVES : 6 - 8   PAN USED : Base & Lid

INGREDIENTS :

¼ cup extra virgin olive oil

2 celery stalks, cut into 1 inch chunks

1 large carrot, cut into 1 inch chunks

1 medium onion, chopped

4 garlic cloves, chopped

1 teaspoon fresh ginger root, grated

1 teaspoon ground turmeric

1 teaspoon sweet paprika

¾ teaspoon ground cinnamon

½ teaspoon ground cumin

½ teaspoon ground black pepper

Pinch of cayenne

2 tablespoons tomato paste

3-15 ounce cans chickpeas, rinsed
and drained

1 cup dry white wine

6 cups chicken stock

1 dried bay leaf

½ cup dried apricots, diced

2 tablespoons preserved lemon, chopped

½ cup cilantro, chopped, more for
garnish

Kosher salt and freshly ground pepper

PREPARATION :

1. Preheat the oven to 350°F. In the Dutch oven, heat the oil over medium heat. Add the celery, carrot and onion. Cook until the onion is translucent, about 6 minutes. Add the garlic, ginger, turmeric, paprika, cinnamon, cumin, black pepper and cayenne, about 1 minute. Make a space in the pan and add the tomato paste there, allowing it to toast for 1 minute before stirring it into the vegetables. Stir in the beans, raise the heat to high, and add the white wine. Boil until the wine is almost evaporated, about 3 minutes.

2. Add the stock and bay leaf into the liquid. Bring to a simmer, cover, and bake for 1 hour. Raise the heat to 400°F, uncover, stir in up to 1 cup water if the stew seems dry, and bake until the stew is crusty on top, about 30 minutes more.

3. Stir in dried apricots, preserved lemon, and chopped cilantro. Season with Kosher salt and freshly ground pepper and serve adding more cilantro for garnish to serve, if desired.

Pro Tip :

You can really stretch a meal out by making big batches, and the Dutch oven is the perfect vessel for that. Leftovers of this stew would work well as a vegetarian taco or burrito filling, filled with rice, avocado slices and plenty of fresh lime wedges on the side.

Shrimp Gumbo

SERVES : 8   PAN USED : Base

INGREDIENTS :

4 slices thick bacon, chopped

1½ pounds shrimp, shells removed and deveined

Kosher salt and freshly ground black pepper

2 links andouille sausage, chopped (about 8 ounces)

Canola oil

⅓ cup all purpose flour

2 celery stalks, chopped (about ½ cup)

1 medium red bell pepper, cored, seeded and chopped

1 medium onion, chopped (about 1 cup)

8 garlic cloves, finely chopped

1 tablespoon tomato paste

2 teaspoons chopped fresh thyme

¼ teaspoon cayenne, or to taste

½ cup dry white wine, optional

6 cups chicken stock

2 dried bay leaves

4 ounces okra, fresh or frozen, trimmed and thinly sliced

1 tablespoon Worcestershire sauce

½ cup scallions (white and green parts) chopped

PREPARATION :

1. Cook the bacon until crispy in Dutch oven over medium heat. Remove and drain on paper towels. Season the shrimp with Kosher salt and freshly ground pepper. Raise the heat to medium and cook the shrimp on both sides, about 1 minute per side, working in batches if necessary. Remove to a plate. Add the sausage and brown all over, about 5 minutes, then reserve on another plate.

2. Add ¼ cup oil to bacon fat. Reduce the heat to medium and stir in the flour with a wooden spoon until smooth. Cook, stirring constantly, until the flour paste smells nutty and is a deep golden brown, about 15 minutes.

3. Add the celery, red pepper, and onion and cook until slightly softened, about 3 minutes. Add the garlic, tomato paste, thyme and cayenne and cook until the garlic is fragrant, about 1 minute. Add the white wine (if using) and bring to a boil. Whisk in the stock and bring to a simmer. Add the bay leaves and okra and return the sausage to the pot. Simmer briskly, about 45 minutes. Remove the bay leaves. Stir in the Worcestershire, reserved bacon, and shrimp. Season with salt, sprinkle with the scallions and serve.

Pro Tip :

A dark brown roux is essential to a good gumbo, so take your time when you brown the flour and oil mixture and stir often to keep it from burning. The flavor should be robust and nutty, a result of the browning process.

DIPS

Pesto White Bean Dip

SERVES : 4   PAN USED : Lid

INGREDIENTS :

½ cup extra-virgin olive oil

6 garlic cloves, crushed

½ teaspoon ground cumin

½ teaspoon smoked paprika

¼ teaspoon crushed red pepper flakes

3 cups cannellini beans cooked and drained

2 lemons, juiced

1 pinch salt

½ cup pesto

2 tablespoons pine nuts, toasted

Pita chips, toasted

Crudite for dipping

PREPARATION :

1. In top pan of Dutch oven, heat the oil and garlic over low heat. Let the garlic gently bubble in the oil until it has softened but hasn't taken on any color, about 5 minutes. Stir in the cumin, paprika, and pepper flakes and let toast until fragrant, about one minute. Remove from the heat and let cool 10 minutes.

2. Add the beans and lemon juice to a food processor. Add the cooked garlic cloves and all but one tablespoon of the spiced oil. Puree to make a smooth dip, season with salt, and puree again. Add pesto and pulse one or two times leaving some swirls of green.

3. Wipe the top pan of Dutch oven clean. Spoon the dip into it and sprinkle with the pine nuts. Drizzle the remaining one tablespoon of spiced oil over the dip and serve.

Pro Tip :

To make a great sandwich filling, cook an additional 1 cup of cannellini beans, drain and lightly crush. Fold into the bean dip at the end. Layer spread on a toasted baguette with thick tomato slices, fresh cucumbers and crisp leafy greens.

Photo on page 49

Spinach and Artichoke Dip

SERVES : 8   PAN USED : Base & Lid

INGREDIENTS :

8 fresh artichokes

One 14-ounce can cannellini beans

1 medium leek, thoroughly cleaned, split and thinly sliced crosswise, (white and light green parts)

1 12-ounce bunch fresh spinach, finely chopped (or 1 10-ounce package frozen spinach, defrosted, drained and finely chopped)

1 tablespoon olive oil

1 cup grated Parmigiano-Reggiano

½ cup heavy cream, plus additional if needed

½ cup sour cream

Kosher salt and freshly ground black pepper

⅓ cup breadcrumbs

1 teaspoon fresh thyme leaves

2 lemons, zested

Fleur de sel, for sprinkling

Baguette slices, toasted

PREPARATION :

1. Bring a small amount of water to a simmer in Dutch oven and set a steamer basket over it. Using a sharp paring knife, peel the stems on the artichokes and remove the tougher outer leaves; remove the inner leaves by hand, then cut away the center chokes. Place the artichokes in the steamer basket, cover and cook until tender when pierced, about 30 minutes, adding hot water if needed during cooking. Roughly chop the artichokes into ½-inch pieces and combine them with the cannellini beans and leeks in a large bowl.

2. Wipe Dutch oven clean, and if using fresh spinach, add olive oil and heat over medium heat. Add spinach and stir constantly until wilted. Add to artichoke mixture.

3. Preheat the oven to 375°F. In a separate bowl, whisk together the Parmigiano-Reggiano, heavy cream and sour cream. Pour into the artichoke mixture and toss well. The mixture should be creamy and smooth; if too thick, add more cream to thin. Sprinkle with Kosher salt and freshly ground pepper.

4. Pour the mixture into lid of Dutch oven. In a small bowl, combine the breadcrumbs, thyme leaves and lemon zest; sprinkle over the top of the casserole.

5. Bake the gratin until the mixture is bubbly and the crust is golden brown, about 30 minutes. Finish with a sprinkle of fleur de sel. Serve with toasted baguette slices.

Pro Tip :

There's no shame in the substitution game. Less time in the kitchen means more time with your friends and family. Substitute two 14 ounce drained cans of artichoke hearts for the fresh ones.

* Photo on page 49

01 French Onion Fondue Dip
Recipe Page 51

01

02   Charred eggplant & Tahini Dip
Recipe Page 50

03   Spinach & Artichoke Dip
Recipe Page 47

04   Pesto White Bean Dip
Recipe Page 46

02

03

04

Charred Eggplant & Tahini Dip

SERVES : 6 - 8   PAN USED : Base & Lid

INGREDIENTS :

2 large eggplant, halved

6 cloves garlic, halved

2 tablespoons extra virgin olive oil, plus additional for drizzling

1 tablespoon unsalted butter

1 teaspoon cumin

2 tablespoons tahini

1 teaspoon lemon zest, finely grated

1 tablespoon fresh lemon juice

Kosher salt

Za'atar for garnish, if available

Pita wedges, toasted

PREPARATION :

1. Preheat oven to 375°F. Using a small knife, make three cross-shaped cuts, deep enough to hold a garlic clove, into the skin of each eggplant. Place half a garlic clove in each cut. Rub the eggplants all over with olive oil and place 2 halfs in top pan, and two halves in Dutch oven, cut side down. Roast until the eggplants are deflated and a knife inserted comes out clean, at least one hour.

2. Allow the eggplants to cool for 15 minutes. Wipe out top pan. Remove the garlic cloves and reserve. Scoop the pulp of the eggplants from their inner skins and place in a colander, allowing it to drain of excess water for at least 15 minutes. Puree the pulp in a food processor with the butter, garlic cloves, tahini, and lemon juice. Season to taste with the Kosher salt. Remove dip from food processor and place back into top pan, smoothing with spatula. Garnish eggplant with a generous sprinkle of Za'atar and a drizzle of extra virgin olive oil. Serve room temperature with toasted pita.

Pro Tip :

This dip would make a great spread as the filling for a vegetarian sandwich. Split a ciabatta loaf in half lengthwise and spread on a thick layer of eggplant dip. Top with large pieces of roasted red peppers, thick slices of buffalo mozzarella, fresh whole basil leaves, a drizzle of olive oil, and generous seasoning of Kosher salt and freshly ground pepper. Wrap in plastic wrap, place a heavy cookbook on top to compress for an hour, and you have a vegetarian muffaletta.

Photo on page 49

French Onion Fondue Dip

SERVES : 8   PAN USED : Base & Lid

INGREDIENTS :

6 bacon strips

4 sweet onions, such as Vidalia, halved and thinly sliced

½ teaspoon sugar

¼ teaspoon Kosher salt

2 tablespoon dry sherry

1 teaspoon chopped fresh thyme

2 cups gruyere cheese, shredded

1 cup sour cream

1 cup mayo

½ teaspoon freshly ground black pepper

Baguette slices, toasted

PREPARATION :

1. Preheat oven to 400°F. Heat Dutch oven over medium heat and cook bacon. Remove to a paper towel lined plate to cool. Crumble.

2. Add onions, sugar, and salt to bacon fat in the Dutch oven and cook over medium-high heat for about 5 minutes. Reduce heat to medium low and cook, stirring often, until onions turn a deep golden brown color. This can take as long as 20-30 minutes.

3. Add sherry and cook 1 minute. Stir in thyme and remove from heat.

4. Mix together sour cream and mayo in a medium bowl. Add crumbled bacon, cheese, onion mixture, and black pepper. Mix together well and transfer to lid of Dutch oven. Bake 20 minutes, or until bubbly and golden brown on top. Serve with toasted baguette slices for dipping.

Pro Tip :

Caramelization takes time. Don't take onions off to early; then you're "blonding" them instead of actually caramelizing them. They should be a rich brown, much reduced from where you started, and very soft but not quite mushy.

* Photo on page 48

Seven Layer Queso Dip

SERVES : 8   PAN USED : Lid

INGREDIENTS :

1 tablespoon vegetable oil

1 medium yellow onion, diced

½ pound ground beef, 80 %

1 large garlic clove

½ teaspoon chipotle chili powder

½ teaspoon paprika

½ teaspoon cumin

1 teaspoon Kosher salt

2 tablespoons sour cream

1 tablespoon tomato paste

1½ cups prepared guacamole

2 jalapeno peppers, seeded and diced

½ cup canned black beans, drained

½ cup frozen corn, drained

1 tomato, seeded and diced

2 tablespoons fresh cilantro, finely chopped

1 ½ cups shredded Mexican cheese mix

2 tablespoons fresh cilantro, chopped fine

Tortilla chips for dipping

1 lime, cut into wedges

PREPARATION :

1. Preheat oven to 350°F. Heat top pan of Dutch oven over medium heat and add vegetable oil. Add onion and saute until transparent.

2. Add ground beef and cook, stirring, until almost cooked through. Mix in garlic, chipotle powder, paprika, cumin and salt and cook until beef is done. Stir in sour cream and tomato paste and remove from heat. Spread beef mixture evenly in pan. Let cool slightly.

3. Dollop guacamole evenly over top of beef layer. Top with jalapenos, beans, corn, and then diced tomato.

4. Spread cheese evenly over the layered vegetables. Place pan in oven and bake for about 20 minutes or until cheese is golden brown and mixture is bubbling. Remove from oven and sprinkle with chopped cilantro.

5. Serve warm with lime wedges and salty tortilla chips.

Pro Tip :

This dish can be assembled up to 24 hours ahead of time. After everything is complete through Step 3, let cool slightly, cover with plastic wrap and place in your refrigerator. The next day, a half hour before your guests arrive, proceed with Steps 4 & 5, layering on the cheese and baking. You'll be more relaxed with some party prep out of the way.

FRIED

Zucchini Hush Puppies

SERVES : 4 - 6   PAN USED : Base

INGREDIENTS :

Canola oil, for frying

1 cup all purpose flour

½ cup fine yellow cornmeal

½ teaspoon baking soda

½ teaspoon Kosher salt, plus more for seasoning the fritters

½ teaspoon cayenne

1 large egg

¾ cup buttermilk

2 cups grated zucchini, wrung very dry in a kitchen towel

¼ cup chopped mixed fresh herbs, such as any combination of basil, chives, cilantro and Italian parsley

PREPARATION :

1. In Dutch oven, heat 2 inches of oil to 360°F. In a large bowl, whisk together the flour, cornmeal, baking soda, salt and cayenne.

2. In a large bowl, whisk together the egg and buttermilk. Whisk in the flour mixture until just combined; don't over mix. Fold in the zucchini and herbs.

3. Using a soup spoon, drop a spoonful of batter (about 1 tablespoon) into the hot oil. It's best to fry these in 2 batches so the temperature of the oil doesn't drop too much (keep the oil between 350°F and 360°F while frying). Fry, flipping once, until golden all over and cooked through, about 4 minutes per batch. Drain on paper towels. Season with salt and serve right away.

Pro Tip :

I use baking soda here to react with the buttermilk, making a light and airy fritter with a slight acidic tang that is a great foil for the sweetness of the vegetables. This well-balanced batter works with most vegetables that can be grated, such as other squash, carrots, sweet potatoes, and also with corn kernels. Just be sure to wring as much liquid as possible out of the grated vegetables before adding to the batter. If using corn, it does not have to be wrung out.

Photo on page 62

Easy Fried Shrimp

SERVES : 8   PAN USED : Base

INGREDIENTS :

Tarter sauce:

1½ cup mayonnaise

2 tablespoon fresh dill, minced

2 tablespoon cornichon, minced

2 tablespoon white wine vinegar

4 teaspoons capers, rinsed and drained, then chopped

2 teaspoon dijon mustard

Kosher salt and freshly ground pepper

Fried shrimp:

2 quarts canola oil

1 cup white rice flour

1 cup IPA style beer

2 pounds large shrimp, peeled and deveined

1 teaspoon freshly cracked black pepper

1 teaspoon Kosher salt

1 lemon, cut into wedges

PREPARATION :

To make the tarter sauce:

1. Place all sauce ingredients in a small bowl and whisk until combined. Refrigerate while preparing the shrimp.

To make the shrimp:

1. Pour the oil into Dutch oven. Heat over medium high heat to 375°F. Line a sheet tray with paper towels and top with a cooling rack.

2. In a medium mixing bowl, whisk together the rice flour and beer until a smooth batter is formed. Season with freshly cracked black pepper and Kosher salt. Holding the tail, dip the shrimp into the batter to evenly coat on both sides. One by one, gently drop the battered shrimp into the preheated oil. Fry for about 1 minute, until golden brown on both sides, flipping once if necessary. While frying the shrimp, be sure to monitor the temperature of the oil and maintain 375°F. Once fried, place the shrimp onto the cooling rack and sprinkle generously with salt.

3. Serve the fried shrimp with tartar sauce for dipping and extra lemon wedges on the side.

Pro Tip :

The heft of a Dutch oven helps retain high temperatures and prevents the heat from fluctuating too much, enabling the oil to cook your food more evenly—and more quickly. The high sides also prevent oil from splattering.

Buffalo Chicken Wings & Blue Cheese Dip

SERVES : 4 - 6   PAN USED : Base

INGREDIENTS :

Blue cheese dip:

4 ounces roquefort or other blue cheese, crumbled

½ cup sour cream

½ cup mayonnaise

¼ cup buttermilk

Chicken wings:

½ cup Frank's hot sauce (or your favorite hot sauce)

Canola oil, for frying

1 cup all purpose flour

1 tablespoon Frank's Dry Rub (or 1 teaspoon each cumin, paprika, garlic powder)

Kosher salt and freshly ground pepper

2½ pounds chicken wings, separated at the joints and patted dry

Celery, cut into sticks

PREPARATION :

To make the blue cheese dip:

1. In a medium bowl, whisk together roquefort, sour cream, mayonnaise, and buttermilk. Set aside while preparing wings.

To make the chicken wings:

1. Put hot sauce in a bowl large enough to hold wings once fried.

2. In Dutch oven, heat 3 inches of oil to 365°F. In a shallow dish, combine the flour and dry rub ingredients. Then season the wings with Kosher salt and freshly ground pepper. Dredge them lightly in the flour mixture and fry, in batches, until golden brown and crispy, about 13 minutes. Drain briefly on paper towels, but add, while still very hot, to the hot sauce. Toss to coat all the wings in the sauce and transfer to a serving platter.

3. Serve wings on platter with a big bowl of the blue cheese dip and a pile of celery sticks.

Pro Tip :

Not feeling spicy? Swap the hot sauce for my Sweet and Tangy BBQ sauce (page 77). Still super delicious with the blue cheese dressing. Don't forget the napkins.

Mini Quinoa Crab Cakes

SERVES : 16 mini crab cakes   PAN USED : Lid

INGREDIENTS :

1 pound jumbo lump crabmeat, picked over for shells

½ cup mayonnaise

¾ cup quinoa, cooked and cooled

½ cup chopped scallions (white and green parts)

1 large egg, beaten

1 tablespoon chopped fresh tarragon

Kosher salt and freshly ground pepper

1¼ cups fine dry bread crumbs, plus more as needed

Canola oil, for frying

1 lemon, finely grated zest and juiced (about 3 tablespoons juice)

Tartar sauce, for dipping

PREPARATION :

1. In a large bowl, combine the crab, mayonnaise, quinoa, scallions, egg, lemon zest and juice, and tarragon. Stir to combine. Season with Kosher salt and freshly ground pepper. Sprinkle with ¼ cup of the bread crumbs and stir them in. You should be able to make a crab cake that holds together but is still a bit wet. If the mixture is too wet to hold together (and it might be, depending on how wet the crab and cooked quinoa are), stir in up to ¼ cup more bread crumbs.

2. Form the mixture into sixteen 1-inch-thick cakes and put on a cookie sheet lined with parchment. Refrigerate for 1 hour to firm them up.

3. When ready to cook the crab cakes, heat ½ inch oil in top pan of Dutch oven and preheat the oven to 250°F. Spread about 1 cup bread crumbs on a plate and lightly dredge the crab cakes in bread crumbs. Fry the crab cakes in 2 batches until golden on both sides and heated through, 3 to 4 minutes per side. Drain the first batch on paper towels and keep them warm in the oven while you cook the second batch. Season the crab cakes with salt and serve with lemon wedges and tartar sauce.

Pro Tip :

When cooking quinoa, think about making a little extra to stretch into another meal. Using leftover quinoa here stretches a pound of crab into 16 hors d'oeuvre size crab cakes. You could also substitute brown rice or even well squeezed cauliflower rice here for the quinoa.

*Zucchini Hush Puppies
Recipe Page 55*

Crispy Scallops with Old Bay Flour

SERVES : 2 - 4   PAN USED : Lid

INGREDIENTS :

½ cup Wondra flour

2 tablespoons old bay seasoning

12 large sea scallops, side muscle or "foot" removed

Kosher salt

Canola oil, for sauteing

3 tablespoons unsalted butter

5 fresh thyme sprigs

½ lemon, juiced (about 1 tablespoon)

PREPARATION :

1. In a small shallow dish, stir together flour and old bay seasoning.

2. Pat the scallops very dry and season with salt. Heat about ½ inch of oil in top pan of Dutch oven over medium-high heat. When the oil is hot, roll the scallops in the old bay flour and add to the skillet. (Depending on the size of your scallops, you may need to do this in 2 batches). Let the scallops cook without moving them until the bottoms are crisp and browned, about 1 ½ minutes. Flip and brown the other side, about 1½ minutes. If your scallops are very large, you may also want to flip them on their rounded sides to brown for 1 minute more. When they're just cooked through, remove the scallops to warmed serving plates.

3. Wipe the top pan of the Dutch oven clean. Melt the butter over medium heat. Add the thyme sprigs and cook until the butter begins to brown, about 2 minutes. Remove from the heat, stir in the lemon juice, and season with salt. Drizzle the butter over the scallops and serve.

Pro Tip :

If you've never cooked scallops before, you'll be asking yourself why after this recipe. They are so quick and delicious and require almost no prep time.

Panko Crusted Pork Chops with Raisin Pear Sauce

SERVES : 2   PAN USED : Lid

INGREDIENTS :

Pork chops:

2 boneless pork chops, about 8 ounces each and 1 inch thick

5 tablespoons Dijon mustard

2 yolks

2 cups Panko bread crumbs

Kosher salt and freshly ground pepper

Raisin pear sauce:

2 tablespoons unsalted butter

1 large shallot, diced

2 teaspoons fresh rosemary, diced

2 teaspoons fresh sage, chopped

½ orange, finely grated zest and juiced (about ½ cup juice)

1 cup chicken stock

2 teaspoons sherry vinegar

½ cup golden raisins

1 ripe bartlett pear, quartered, core removed and sliced thin

¼ cup capers, drained

1 tablespoon dijon mustard

1 tablespoon Italian parsley, chopped

PREPARATION :

To make the pork chops:

1. Put the bread crumbs in a shallow dish wide enough for coating and season with Kosher salt and freshly ground pepper. In another dish, mix the mustard and yolks together. Brush the chops with the mustard mixture and dredge all over in the crumbs.

2. Heat lid of Dutch oven over medium heat and add the oil. When the oil is hot, brown the chops on both sides, about 2 minutes per side. Remove them to a plate and wipe out pan.

To make the sauce:

1. Heat lid of Dutch oven over medium heat. Add the butter, and when the butter is melted, add the shallot and cook until fragrant, about 1 minute. Add the orange zest and juice and chicken stock and bring to a boil. Add the vinegar, raisins, pear, and capers. Simmer until the sauce is reduced by half, about 5 minutes. Whisk in the mustard and parsley.

2. Put the chops on top of the raisin pear sauce and bake until the chops are just cooked through, about 8-10 minutes.

Pro Tip :

The more you use your cast iron, the more history it acquires. It is so versatile and you can cook everything from breakfast to dinner, and many meals in between. Cook in it all day and often, like my mom did with these pork chops. Everytime you heat the pan, it will evoke memories of your favorite dishes and the people you shared them with.

Chicken Paillard with Arugula Salad

SERVES : 4   PAN USED : Base & Lid

INGREDIENTS :

Chicken:

4 skin-on, boneless chicken breasts (each about 6 ounces)

Kosher salt and freshly ground pepper

2 cups all-purpose flour

1 tablespoon smoked paprika

½ teaspoon garlic powder

½ teaspoon onion powder

Canola oil, for sauteing

4 tablespoons butter, unsalted (½ stick)

4 sprigs fresh thyme

4 sprigs fresh rosemary

4 garlic cloves

Arugula Dressing:

1 garlic clove, finely chopped

1 tablespoon dijon mustard

2 tablespoons champagne vinegar

1 tablespoons fresh lemon juice

1 tablespoons maple syrup

¼ teaspoon salt

¼ teaspoon freshly ground black pepper

¼ cup extra virgin olive oil

4 cups arugula, or mixed greens

Shaved Pecorino cheese

PREPARATION :

To make the dressing:

1. In a small bowl combine garlic, mustard, champagne vinegar, lemon juice, maple syrup, Kosher salt and freshly ground pepper. While whisking, stream in olive oil until dressing is emulsified. Set aside.

To make the chicken:

1. Preheat the oven to 400°F. One at a time, put the chicken breasts between 2 sheets of plastic wrap and flatten to an even ½ to ¾ -inch thickness with a meat mallet. Season the chicken with salt.

2. In a large shallow dish, stir together the flour, paprika, garlic powder, and onion powder. Season with salt. Dredge the skin side of the chicken breasts in the flour mixture.

3. Heat the lid and the Dutch oven over medium high heat. Depending on the size of the chicken breasts, you may need to use both pans, and if so, simply divide the ingredients between the skillets and cook simultaneously. Add enough oil to film the bottom of the pan (s). When the oil just begins to smoke lightly, add the dredged chicken, skin side down, and shake the pan to make sure the chicken doesn't stick. Cook until the skin begins to brown, about 3 minutes.

4. Transfer the chicken to the oven and cook until the skin is very brown and crispy, about 5 minutes. Remove from the oven, flip the skin side up, and add the butter, thyme, rosemary, and garlic (or divide between the 2 skillets). Return to the oven and cook until the chicken is just cooked through, about 3 minutes.

5. Dress salad greens lightly and season with Kosher salt and freshly ground pepper. Top chicken paillard with a big heap of arugula salad and shave fresh pecorino on top.

Pro Tip :

This method of cooking lightly floured chicken breasts over quick heat high is a perfect fit for cast iron. It was built for this type of dish. You'll agree when you bite into the shatteringly crisp skin.

Spring Vegetable Tempura with Matcha Sea Salt

SERVES : 8   PAN USED : Base

INGREDIENTS :

2 quarts canola oil

1½ pounds of your favorite tender spring vegetables, peeled and trimmed (asparagus, baby carrots, ramps, fiddleheads, sugar snap peas, or baby artichokes)

1¼ cups flour

¾ cup cornstarch

1 tablespoon baking powder

1½ tablespoon sugar

Pinch of salt

3½ cups ice water

1 tablespoon sea salt

1 teaspoon matcha powder

PREPARATION :

1. Fill Dutch oven with canola oil and heat to 350°F.

2. While oil is heating, prepare vegetables for dipping. Trim any tough ends or peel where necessary. Set aside on tray.

3. Prepare matcha salt by mixing salt and matcha powder. Set aside.

4. Combine flour, cornstarch, baking powder and sugar. Slowly pour 3½ cups ice water to the dry ingredient mixture and then gently fold until almost smooth. Do not overwork.

5. Taking one vegetable at a time, dip into the tempura batter. Immediately drop into the oil and fry until golden brown, about 45 seconds to one minute. Drain the tempura on a wire rack over paper towels. Continue with remaining vegetables. Serve hot with a sprinkle of matcha salt.

Pro Tip :

This batter can also be used to coat fish. Cut 2 ounce portions of Atlantic Cod and dip in the batter. Fry until golden brown, drain on towels and season with salt. Use the tartar sauce recipe from our Easy Fried Shrimp recipe for dipping!

ZAKARIAN FAMILY FAVORITES

Ham Steak Sandwiches

SERVES : 4   PAN USED : Lid

INGREDIENTS :

1 ham steak, 1 pound

¼ cup maple syrup

1 tablespoon apple cider vinegar

1 tablespoon dijon mustard

1 tablespoon unsalted butter

4 eggs, large

Parker House Rolls

PREPARATION :

1. Mix together maple syrup, vinegar and mustard in small bowl. Brush one side of ham steak with mixture and place glazed side down in top pan of Dutch oven over medium heat. Brush top of ham steak. Cook over medium heat, about 5 minutes on each side, or until cooked through and glaze has thickened. Remove ham steaks to a cutting board.

2. Return pan to heat and add 1 tablespoon of butter. Crack eggs into pan and cook approximately 1½ - 2 minutes per side for an over easy egg.

3. Cut ham steak into pieces that will fit on the bottom of your roll. Top each with an over easy egg and season with additional Kosher salt and freshly ground pepper.

Pro Tip :

Don't have a huge family coming over for the holidays? Instead of having to buy a whole ham, a ham steak will still satisfy that traditional craving on a budget. Any leftovers can be cubed and added to soups or stews.

Olive Oil Poached Tuna with Braised Bok Choy

SERVES : 4   PAN USED : Base & Lid

INGREDIENTS :

4 pieces of fresh tuna, 1 inch thick, skinned

4 cups extra virgin olive oil

2 sprigs thyme

I fresh bay leaf

I head garlic, cut in half

4 shallots, peeled and sliced thin

1 tablespoon whole coriander seeds

1 tablespoon whole fennel seeds

Kosher salt and freshly ground black pepper

Braised bok choy:

3 small heads bok choy

2 tablespoons unsalted butter

1 knob of ginger, cut into slices

1 teaspoon Kosher salt

½ teaspoon freshly ground white pepper

⅓ cup dry white wine

1½ cups chicken stock

PREPARATION :

1. Season the tuna on both sides with Kosher salt and freshly ground pepper, then sprinkle with the anise seeds. Place the seasoned tuna on a plate, cover with plastic wrap, and cure in the refrigerator for about 40 minutes. Meanwhile, place the oil, thyme, bay leaf, garlic, shallots, coriander seeds and fennel seeds in Dutch oven. Season the oil lightly with Kosher salt and freshly ground pepper, and bring it to a gentle simmer over medium heat. Reduce the heat to low and cook for 30 minutes.

2. Cut the bok choy in quarters, or halves if they are small, then slice them lengthwise, about ½ inch thick. Melt the butter over medium heat in top pan of Dutch oven with ginger slices. Add the bok choy slices, season with the Kosher salt and freshly ground pepper, and brown evenly on both side, 12 to 15 minutes. Add the wine and simmer until the pan is almost dry. Add the stock and raise the heat to bring it to a simmer. Reduce the heat slightly and braise for about 20 minutes. Turn the bok choy slices over and continue to braise until they are tender, about 15 minutes more. Remove the bok choy from the braising liquid and reserve. Raise the heat to medium high and reduce the braising liquid until it thickens to your preference, 5 to 10 minutes. Reserve sauce.

3. About 15 minutes before you plan to serve the dish, heat the seasoned 4 cups of poaching oil to a steady temperature of 160 to 175°F; at this temperature, it will not simmer but occasional small bubbles will appear. Use a spatula to gently slide the tuna fillets the oil. Poach until the fish is almost cooked through, about 5 minutes.

4. To serve, place one piece of tuna on a plate. Spoon a piece of braised bok choy and some of the braising sauce next to it, drizzling over both the tuna and the bok choy.

Pro Tip :

Poaching fish in olive oil is one of the gentler cooking processes. It can be thought of as an "instant confit"- nothing is lost, and the fish retains its moist essence. Be sure to use a high quality olive oil here, it lends a delicious perfume without penetrating the fish and rendering it heavy and oily.

* Butter Braised Asparagus with Lemon Sauce & Feta Recipe
Page 117

Minute Steak Tagliata with Wild Mushroom Ragout

SERVES : 2 - 4   PAN USED : Lid

INGREDIENTS :

Mushroom ragout:

2 tablespoons extra virgin olive oil

1 small clove fresh garlic, minced

1 shallot, minced

¾ cup shiitake mushroom, sliced

¾ cup cremini mushroom, sliced

¾ cup oyster mushrooms, sliced

1 sprig fresh thyme, minced

1 sprig tarragon, minced

¼ cup dry red wine

2 tablespoons unsalted butter

Kosher salt and freshly ground pepper to taste

Steak:

1 teaspoon freshly ground black pepper

1 teaspoon celery salt

1 teaspoon sugar

¼ teaspoon cayenne

1 hanger steak (about 1 ¾ pounds)

2 tablespoons extra virgin olive oil

PREPARATION :

To make steak:

1. In a small bowl, combine the pepper, celery salt, sugar, and cayenne. Rub the mixture all over the steak and then drizzle with the oil and rub again to coat the steak. Wrap in plastic and let marinate in the refrigerator for at least 8 hours or overnight. Remove the steak from refrigerator 30 minutes before you're ready to cook to come to room temperature.

To make mushroom ragout:

1. Using the lid of the Dutch oven, heat olive oil to just before smoking and add mushrooms, thyme, tarragon, salt, pepper, garlic, and shallots. Stir mushrooms continuously over heat until they begin to release moisture and start showing liquid in bottom of pan, about 2-4 minutes. Add wine and cook until three quarters of liquid has been reabsorbed. Cook for another 2-3 minutes to thicken remaining liquid and whisk in butter. Set aside while you are cooking the steak.

2. Heat lid of Dutch oven to medium high heat. Grill steak, turning once, until the internal temperature reads 125°F, for medium rare, about 5-6 minutes on each side. Let rest on a cutting board 10 minutes before slicing.

3. To serve, slice against the grain and serve with mushroom ragout.

Pro Tip :

A cast iron skillet is excellent for searing meat because it gets extremely hot and maintains a consistent temperature through the surface of the pan, giving an even delecious dark brown crust on the surface of the meat. Using high-temperature cooking with cast iron produces these complex flavors. So when it's too cold outside to heat up the grill, get out the cast iron!

Shrimp Scampi

SERVES : 6 - 8   PAN USED : Lid

INGREDIENTS :

1 stick unsalted butter, room temperature

2 teaspoons Italian Flat leaf parsley, chopped

2 teaspoons Tarragon, chopped

3 pounds extra large shrimp, tail shells left on, and butterflied

2 tablespoons all-purpose flour, for dusting

½ cup extra-virgin olive oil

1 teaspoon freshly ground black pepper, plus more to taste

4 cloves garlic, minced

¾ cup dry white wine

2 lemons, juiced (about 6 tablespoons)

¼ cup chicken stock

Italian flat leaf parsley, chopped for garnish

tarragon, chopped for garnish

Cooked pasta or crusty bread

PREPARATION :

1. Place the butter, parsley and tarragon in a bowl. Use a fork to mix until well combined. Place the butter on a sheet of plastic wrap and form it into a 1-inch log. Enclose the log in the plastic wrap, then put it in the refrigerator until it is thoroughly chilled.

2. Pat the shrimp dry, then lightly dust with the flour. Working in batches, heat 2 tablespoons of oil in lid of Dutch oven over medium high heat. Add only as many shrimp as fit into the pan in a single, uncrowded layer (Expect to cook three or four batches). Season the shrimp with the Kosher salt and freshly ground pepper. Cook the shrimp, turning them so they are golden on both sides and nearly cooked through, about 3 minutes per batch. Transfer the shrimp to a large plate lined with paper towels to drain any excess oil.

3. Once the shrimp are browned, wipe the lid clean. Add about 1 tablespoon of oil and adjust the heat to medium low. Add the garlic and cook, stirring frequently, until it is soft and fragrant, about 1 minute. Add the wine, lemon juice, and stock, raise the heat to medium, and bring the liquid to a simmer. Cook the sauce until it is reduced by about two thirds, 4 to 5 minutes.

4. Cut the chilled herb butter into small pieces and whisk it into the sauce one piece at a time. Season the sauce with Kosher salt and freshly ground pepper to taste. Return the shrimp to the pan and cook, stirring, until heated through and well coated with sauce. Season with additional Kosher salt and freshly ground pepper to taste. Transfer the shrimp to a platter, sprinkle additional minced parsley and tarragon on top, and serve immediately with spaghetti and crusty bread.

Pro Tip :

The even heat that is inherent to cast iron is perfect for cooking small shellfish. Once the shrimp are added to the pan, the trick is to cook them just long enough that they turn pink all over,.

Beef Bolognese

SERVES : 8 - 10   PAN USED : Base & Lid

INGREDIENTS :

1½ pounds ground chuck

1½ pounds ground veal

½ pound ground Italian sausage

2 white onions, chopped

2 peeled carrots, chopped

6 garlic cloves, sliced

½ cup tomato paste

3 inch chunk pecorino rind

¼ cup olive oil

1 cup red wine

2 cups beef stock

1 fresh thyme and 1 rosemary bunch, tied

2-28 ounce cans San Marzano tomatoes, crushed

Freshly cooked spaghetti for serving

Shaved pecorino romano, for serving

PREPARATION :

1. Heat Dutch oven over high heat. Add all meat and cook until very well browned. Remove meat from pan and set aside on plate, keeping the fat.

2. Grind all vegetables in food processor until size of small pebble. Add to beef fat and sweat until very soft and lightly brown. Add back beef and any juices on plate. Add tomato paste and sweat out the tomatoes, cooking for about 10 minutes.

3. Add wine and reduce by half. Add beef stock, tomatoes, herbs and romano rinds.

4. Cover and simmer slowly, approximately one hour and thirty minutes, or until thickened and reduced.

5. Finish with spaghetti and grated Romano cheese.

Pro Tip :

Bolognese tastes even better the next day so take your time enjoying the cooking process and knowing that you've planned ahead for tomorrow's dinner. This recipe makes a generous amount of sauce, freeze any leftovers within 3 days, and you'll have a hearty dinner on hand.

BBQ Chicken Sandwich

SERVES : 8 - 10   PAN USED : Base & Lid

INGREDIENTS :

BBQ Sauce:

1 tablespoon canola oil

3 medium white onions, finely chopped (about 5 cups)

3 garlic cloves garlic, finely chopped

1 teaspoon ground cumin

½ teaspoon smoked paprika

1 cup tomato paste

4 canned chipotle peppers plus their sauce

1 tablespoon anchovy paste

1 quart unseasoned chicken stock

1 cup cider vinegar

1 cup maple syrup

½ cup orange juice concentrate

½ cup dijon mustard

½ cup molasses

1 tablespoon fish sauce

¼ cup Worcestershire sauce, plus 2 tablespoons to finish

Kosher salt and freshly ground black pepper, to taste

Chicken:

8 boneless, skinless chicken thighs

Sesame seed rolls

PREPARATION :

To make the sauce:

1. In Dutch oven over low heat, heat the canola oil. When oil is hot, add the onions and garlic, slowly sweating them until tender but not colored, about 20 minutes. Add the cumin, smoked paprika, tomato paste, chipotles, and anchovy paste. Sweat over low heat another 5 minutes, taking care not to scorch. Add the stock, vinegar, maple syrup, orange juice concentrate, mustard, molasses, fish sauce, and ¼ cup of the Worcestershire sauce. Simmer over low heat until thick and silky, about 50 minutes to 1 hour. Adjust the seasoning with Kosher salt and freshly ground pepper. Stir in the remaining 2 tablespoons of Worcestershire. Cook until barbecue sauce is thickened and coats the back of a spoon, about 30 minutes.

To make the chicken:

1. Preheat oven to 350°F. Season chicken thighs with Kosher salt and freshly ground pepper. Heat top pan of Dutch oven over medium heat with 2 tablespoons of oil to pan. Working in two batches, brown both sides of chicken, removing to a plate as you go. Add all of the chicken to the bbq sauce in the Dutch oven. Wipe out lid of Dutch oven, and use to cover the base, baking for 30 - 40 minutes, or until chicken is cooked through.

2. Remove Dutch oven and take lid off. Remove chicken from sauce and let cool slightly. Shred chicken with forks and then return to pot. Serve big scoops of bbq chicken on buttered, toasted sesame buns.

Pro Tip :

Slather this diverse barbecue sauce on everything from your favorite smoked ribs to barbecue chicken wings. It holds well, and even freezes so go ahead and double up on a batch. It's more economical than store bought, and of course tastier.

Steamed Mussels with Lime Broth

SERVES : 6 - 8   PAN USED : Base & Lid

INGREDIENTS :

5 shallots, peeled and sliced thin

1 teaspoon coriander seeds

1 knob fresh turmeric, sliced

1 teaspoon turmeric powder

2 lime leaves, bruised

1 teaspoon black peppercorns

1 cup muscat or sweet white wine

1 cup dry white wine

2 limes, juiced

4 cups fish stock

¾ cup coconut milk

½ cup heavy cream

Kosher salt and freshly ground pepper

24 P.E.I. mussels (cleaned)

1 bunch Italian parsley, washed, cut into chiffonade

1 beefsteak tomato, peeled, seeded and diced small

2 large cloves garlic, sliced paper thin, blanched

Sweet garlic butter:

10 tablespoons unsalted butter

10 cloves garlic

2 cups whole milk

⅓ cup parsley, chopped

PREPARATION :

1. In Dutch oven, over medium heat, sweat shallots, coriander, fresh turmeric, turmeric powder, lime leaves, and peppercorn until shallots are translucent. Deglaze with juice of 1 lime and both wines and reduce until almost dry. Add in fish stock and reduce by half. Add coconut milk and heavy cream and reduce by half. Season with salt, freshly ground pepper and lime juice. Strain and reserve over very low heat in a separate pan.

2. For the garlic butter, place garlic cloves in the lid of Dutch oven with milk and simmer until garlic is very soft. Strain off half of the milk and discard. Place strained garlic and milk into food processor and puree until smooth. Add butter and puree again until smooth. Fold in chopped parsley. Clean out top pan top prepare for the next step.

3. In Dutch oven, over medium heat, put half of the butter puree with the mussels. Sweat uncovered for a minute then pour in the warm broth from the first part of the recipe. Cover with top pan and cook mussels until they all open, just a few minutes. Add in remaining butter, parsley, tomato and blanched garlic slices. Serve warm with baguette slices.

Pro Tip :

Mussels are the ultimate easy summer food! They are simple to make and incredibly versatile. Once you learn the basic method of cooking, you can create many new flavors. Just remember, discard any mussels that do not open.

Weeknight Chicken Picatta

SERVES : 4   PAN USED : Lid

INGREDIENTS :

2 boneless chicken breast, butterflied and then cut in half

Kosher salt and freshly ground black pepper

All-purpose flour, for dredging

3 tablespoons unsalted butter

3 tablespoons extra-virgin olive oil

1 large shallot, finely minced

2 cups chicken stock

½ cup dry white wine (such as a Sauvignon Blanc)

1 lemon, juice and zest

3 tablespoons brined capers

2 tablespoons fresh parsley, chopped

PREPARATION :

1. Season chicken with Kosher salt and freshly ground pepper. Dredge chicken in flour and shake off excess. In top pan of Dutch oven over medium high heat, melt butter and olive oil. When butter and oil start to sizzle, add 2 pieces of chicken and cook for about 3 minutes on each side, or until cooked through. Repeat with remaining chicken. Remove chicken to plate.

2. Heat the lid of the Dutch oven with the drippings over medium heat. Add the shallots and cook until soft and lightly caramelized, about 5 minutes. Add the white wine and reduce until the pan begins to sizzle again, 2-3 minutes. Add the chicken stock and reduce by one-half, about 7-8 minutes. Add the capers and parsley, then whisk in the butter and lemon zest and juice. Season with Kosher salt and freshly ground pepper.

3. Immediately spoon pan sauce over warm chicken.

Pro Tip :

This is a very quick weeknight dinner that will please the whole family. The most important part of this recipe is using a hot pan, which makes it perfect for cast iron. You won't have to stand there watching it reduce all day. If you don't have stock, just use water. Pan sauce like a pro!

Grilled Salmon with Green Goddess Sauce

SERVES : 4   PAN USED : Lid

INGREDIENTS :

Green goddess sauce:

1 avocado, pit removed and cut into large chunks

⅔ cup plain greek yogurt, full fat

⅓ cup mayonnaise

2 garlic cloves

¼ cup parsley, chopped

¼ cup basil, chopped

2 tablespoons chives, minced

2 tablespoons dill, chopped, plus fronds for garnish

½ lemon, juiced

Kosher salt and freshly ground pepper

Salmon:

4 skin-on center-cut salmon fillets (each about 6 ounces)

Canola oil

Kosher salt and freshly ground pepper

PREPARATION :

To make the green goddess sauce:

1. Add all ingredients to a food processor and blend until combined. Cover and set aside while you cook the salmon.

To make the salmon:

1. Heat the lid of Dutch oven over high heat. Brush the pan and the salmon with oil. Season the salmon with Kosher salt and freshly ground pepper. Grill, skin side down, until the skin is crispy, and then flip and grill on the other side until just cooked through, about 4 minutes per side. Spoon a big spoonful on bottom of plate and spread to cover. With spatula, gently place a piece of salmon on top of the sauce. Garnish with dill fronds.

Pro Tip :

Turn leftovers into a salad the next day. Layer green bibb lettuce on your plate, break up chunks of cold salmon, and top with green goddess sauce. You may have to thin out the sauce a little for a dressing like consistency with a bit more lemon. Add some shaved red onion and capers and you have a satisfying and filling dinner!

ROASTED, BRAISED AND BAKED

Roasted Chicken with Crispy Smashed Garlic Potatoes & Gravy

SERVES : 2   PAN USED : Base

INGREDIENTS :

Potatoes and chicken:

10 red potatoes

2 tablespoons olive oil

3 small garlic cloves, minced

½ cup salted butter, room temperature

1½ teaspoons Italian flat leaf parsley, minced

1½ teaspoons fresh thyme, minced

1 small clove garlic, minced

Grated zest of ½ lemon

½ teaspoon Kosher salt

¼ teaspoon freshly ground pepper

1 3 ½-4 pound chicken, preferably organic

Olive oil

Gravy:

¼ cup drippings from roast chicken

2½ tablespoons all-purpose flour

2 cups chicken stock, or more if needed

Kosher salt and freshly ground black pepper to taste

PREPARATION :

1. Preheat oven to 400°F. Fill your Dutch oven halfway with water. Liberally salt the water and bring to boil. Add red potatoes, and boil for 15 minutes, or until they are fork tender. Strain; set aside potatoes. Wipe Dutch oven dry and drizzle bottom with the olive oil. Gently and loosely smash cooked potatoes and add to the bottom of Dutch oven. Season with Kosher salt, fresh pepper and chopped garlic.

2. Place the butter, parsley, thyme, garlic and lemon zest in a small mixing bowl; stir to combine. Season generously with Kosher salt and freshly ground pepper. Using your fingers and starting at the back end of the chicken, loosen the skin from the breast, leaving the skin nearest the neck opening attached. Spread the butter mixture under the skin. Season the cavity lightly with Kosher salt and freshly ground pepper.

3. Place the chicken on top of the potatoes in the Dutch oven and season it on the outside lightly with Kosher salt and freshly ground pepper. Place the chicken in the oven to roast for 15 minutes. Reduce the temperature to 350°F, and continue to roast until an instant-read thermometer inserted in a thigh registers 155°F, or the thigh juices run clear, 45-55 minutes. Remove from pan and allow the chicken to rest in a warm place for 20 minutes.

4. Meanwhile, make the gravy. Pour off all but ¼ cup pan drippings from Dutch oven, then cook over medium-high heat until deep golden, 1 to 2 minutes. Add flour and cook, stirring constantly, 1 minute. Stir in stock and simmer, stirring and scraping up brown bits, until thickened, about 3 to 4 minutes. Whisk in 4 tablespoons butter then strain through a fine strainer into a bowl.

5. Carve the chicken and transfer the meat to a large platter. Serve with crispy potatoes and gravy.

Pro Tip :

A key to the roast chicken process is the 20 minute resting time, which keeps the juices from running out when you carve the chicken. Loosely tent with foil if you are concerned about the chicken retaining heat while resting.

Red Wine Braised Short Ribs with Creamy Polenta

SERVES : 6   PAN USED : Base & Lid

INGREDIENTS :

Short ribs:

4 tablespoons extra virgin olive oil

3 white onions, cut into eighths

4 medium carrots, cut into thick slices

2 large leeks, washed thoroughly and cut into thick slices

2 teaspoon Kosher salt

4 heads of garlic, halved crosswise

2 tablespoons coriander seeds

2 tablespoons black peppercorns

1 teaspoon thyme, finely chopped

½ teaspoon rosemary, finely chopped

2 fresh bay leaves

2 cups beef stock

2 cups red wine

6 thick center-cut short ribs, bone-in, each about ¾ pound

Polenta:

2 cups whole milk

2 cups chicken stock or low-sodium broth

2 tablespoons unsalted butter

1 cup instant polenta (about 7 ounces)

½ cup heavy cream

1 tablespoon mascarpone cheese

½ teaspoon finely chopped rosemary

½ teaspoon finely chopped thyme

1 tablespoon freshly grated Parmesan cheese, plus more for serving

Kosher salt and freshly ground pepper

Photo on Page 91

PREPARATION :

To make the short ribs:

1. Preheat the oven to 375°F. Heat Dutch oven over medium heat with 2 tablespoons of oil. When Dutch oven is hot, but not smoking, add the onions, carrots, leeks and 1 teaspoon of the salt. Cook, stirring occasionally, until the vegetables are soft, about 15 minutes. Add the garlic, 2 tablespoons of the coriander seeds, the peppercorns, thyme, rosemary, and bay leaves.

2. Season the short ribs with 1 teaspoon of the salt and add them to the pan. Pour in beef stock and wine to just cover the ribs and bring to a simmer. Transfer the Dutch oven to the oven. Simmer the ribs, turning them every 30 minutes, until they are tender, about 2 hours.

3. Once braised, remove the ribs to a plate. Let the braising liquid cool so the grease floats to the top. Skim and discard the grease with a large spoon. Place the Dutch oven with degreased braising liquid over medium-high heat. Bring it to a boil and cook until it is reduced to your liking. Use the reduced braising liquid as a sauce for the ribs and polenta.

To make the polenta:

1. In lid of Dutch oven, combine the milk, stock and butter and bring to a boil. Whisk (with a silicone coated whisk) in the polenta and cook over moderate heat, stirring constantly with a wooden spoon until thick, about 8 minutes. Remove from the heat and stir in the heavy cream, mascarpone, herbs and Parmesan. Season with Kosher salt and freshly ground pepper.

Pro Tip :

While short ribs can be served immediately, they are a fatty cut, which makes the dish very rich. I prefer to let the ribs sit in the sauce and cool to room temperature, then cover and refrigerate them overnight. At this point, you can scrape away the hardened layer of fat from the top before reheating. They will also improve in flavor and tenderness while resting overnight.

Braised Veal Shank

SERVES : 6   PAN USED : Base & Lid

INGREDIENTS :

3 tablespoons ground cumin

3 tablespoons ground coriander

2 tablespoons Madras curry powder

2 tablespoons fresh rosemary, minced

2 tablespoons fresh thyme, minced

2 tablespoons garlic, minced

1 tablespoon black pepper, coarsely ground, plus more to taste

½ cup plus 2 tablespoons extra virgin olive oil

1 tablespoon Kosher salt, plus more to taste

6 veal shanks (1 to 1¼ pounds each), trimmed of excess fat

2 stalks celery, coarsely chopped

1 large yellow onion, coarsely chopped

1 large carrot, coarsely chopped

1 cup dry white wine

2 quarts chicken stock

PREPARATION :

1. Marinate the veal shanks. Place the cumin, coriander, curry powder, rosemary, thyme, garlic, and pepper in a small mixing bowl, and stir to combine. Stir in 6 tablespoons of the oil to make a paste. Season the paste with 1 tablespoon salt. Rub the veal shanks with the spice rub, place them in a dish, and cover with plastic wrap (or in a ziploc bag), and refrigerate overnight.

2. The next day preheat the oven to 350°F. Wipe the spice paste from the shanks with a paper towel and discard. Heat 2 tablespoons of the oil in Dutch oven over medium heat. Working in batches if necessary, brown the shanks on all sides, about 20 minutes. Wipe out the Dutch oven, removing any burned spices. Add the remaining 2 tablespoons of oil with the celery, onion, and carrot, and cook over medium heat until the vegetables begin to soften and brown, about 12 minutes.

3. Return the shanks to the Dutch oven, add the wine, and simmer until the pan is almost dry, about 8 minutes. Add the stock and bring to a simmer. Cover the Dutch oven with the lid and place it in the oven to braise for 1 hour. Turn the shanks and cook until the veal is very tender, about 1 more hour. Remove the pan from the oven and allow the shanks to cook in their cooking liquid.

4. Transfer the shanks to a plate and pass the braising liquid through a strainer back into Dutch oven. Discard the solids. Bring the braising liquid to a simmer over medium high heat. Skim the fat as it rises. (Alternatively, chill the sauce so the fat hardens on top and can be removed). Reduce the braising liquid to about 2 cups of sauce, approximately 15 minutes. Season the sauce with Kosher salt and freshly ground pepper to taste. Return the shanks back to the Dutch oven. Pour the sauce over the shanks and reheat in the oven, basting with sauce frequently. Serve the shanks on a platter or in large bowls topped with sauce.

Pro Tip :

This is a great meal to prep ahead of time! Like most braised or stewed meat dishes, this one improves if left in the fridge for a day or two and served reheated. This dish pairs perfectly with a hearty bottle of red wine.

Spinach Gratin Recipe Page 116

Cider Brined Pork Roast

SERVES : 4 - 6   PAN USED : Base & Lid

INGREDIENTS :

Pork:

3-4 pound bone in pork roast

4 cups water

1 cup sugar

½ cup Kosher salt

1 quarts apple cider

Freshly ground black pepper

Extra virgin olive oil, for searing the pork

Chicken stock, as needed (up to 2 cups)

Sauce:

2 tablespoons unsalted butter

1 large shallot, finely chopped

1 tablespoon all-purpose flour

1 small orange, zested

¼ teaspoon smoked paprika

2 fresh bay leaves

Splash of sherry vinegar

Kosher salt and freshly ground pepper

PREPARATION :

1. To make the brine, the day before you make the pork, combine 2 cups cider, granulated sugar, and ½ cup salt in Dutch oven; bring to a boil, stirring until sugar and salt dissolve. Add water and remaining 2 cups cider; cool to room temperature. Add pork; refrigerate overnight, turning occasionally.

2. Preheat the oven to 425°F. Remove the pork from marinade and let it come to room temperature while the oven preheats. Season the pork with Kosher salt and freshly ground pepper.

3. Heat the lid of Dutch oven over medium-high heat. Add a thin film of olive oil and sear the pork to brown on all sides, about 4 minutes in all. Transfer the pork to your Dutch oven, but reserve the top to make the sauce. Roast the pork, bones up, for 15 minutes at 425°F. Add ¾ cup water to the pan, then reduce the oven temperature to 350°F, and roast until the internal temperature of the pork is 145°F, about 40 to 45 minutes longer, adding up to another ¾ cup of water to the pan to keep the drippings in the bottom from burning. Let rest on a cutting board while you make the sauce. Pour the drippings into a bowl and remove top layer of fat. Pour into a measuring cup and add enough chicken stock to make 2 cups in all.

4. Over medium heat, heat the lid used to sear the pork. Add 1 tablespoon of the butter and the shallot and cook until the shallots are softened, about 3 minutes. Sprinkle the flour over and stir to combine. Cook 1 to 2 minutes, then add the orange zest and paprika. Pour in the stock, add the bay leaves, and bring to a rapid simmer. Simmer until slightly thickened and reduced by approximately **one third**, about 5 minutes. Remove the bay leaves, whisk in the remaining tablespoon of butter, and add a splash of sherry vinegar. Season sauce with Kosher salt and freshly ground pepper.

5. Carve the roast, between the bones, into 4 portions. Ladle about ¼ cup of sauce over each serving and pass the rest of the sauce at the table.

Pro Tip :

The leftover pork makes for an excellent base in a sandwich. Just add mustard, mayo, and red onion and serve between two pieces of country toast.

Shepherd's Pie

SERVES : 8   PAN USED : Base

INGREDIENTS :

Filling:

2 pounds ground beef

½ teaspoon salt

½ teaspoon black pepper

1 tablespoon olive oil

1 large onion chopped

1 pound carrots, peeled and chopped

2 stalks celery, chopped

4 cloves garlic

1 pound bag frozen green peas

¼ cup tomato paste

1 tablespoon fresh rosemary, chopped

½ tablespoon fresh thyme, chopped

½ tablespoon fresh oregano, chopped

1 tablespoon fresh parsley

2 tablespoons Worcestershire sauce

2 cups beef broth

3 tablespoons all-purpose flour

Topping:

4 large russet potatoes

1 cup chicken broth

⅓ cup sour cream

½ teaspoon salt

½ teaspoon pepper

1 teaspoon paprika

⅓ cup grated cheddar cheese

3 tablespoons shaved Parmesan cheese

PREPARATION :

1. Wash potatoes, scrubbing well. Peel skins off and cut potatoes into about 1 inch sized chunks. Fill Dutch oven with water about half way up and season with about 1 teaspoon salt. Bring to a boil. Add potatoes to water and boil until softened, about 20 minutes. Drain and wipe out Dutch oven. Place potatoes in large bowl and mash with the chicken broth, sour cream, salt, and pepper. Stir until very well combined and set aside.

2. Preheat oven to 400°F. Heat Dutch oven over medium-high heat. Add ground beef and season with Kosher salt and freshly ground pepper. Cook until browned, about 5 minutes. Remove from heat and drain excess fat. Add olive oil to pan. Add onion, carrots, celery and garlic. Saute until softened, about 7 minutes.

3. Add frozen peas to Dutch oven and saute for 2 minutes. Stir tomato paste into mixture in pan until well combined. Add rosemary, thyme, oregano, parsley, Worcestershire sauce, and beef broth. Stir very well. Sprinkle flour evenly over mixture while constantly stirring. Reduce to simmer and let simmer for at least 10 minutes, stirring occasionally.

4. Remove Dutch oven from stove and spread mashed potatoes evenly over topping. Sprinkle paprika over potatoes, followed by cheddar and Parmesan cheeses. Bake for 25-35 minutes or until bubbling all over and the cheese has browned.

Pro Tip :

Make dinner time less stressful by assembling this dish the night before. The meat mixture and mashed potatoes can be made ahead of time and assembled without the cheese. Just add a little extra baking time, about 15 - 20 minutes.

Chicken, Sausage and Bean Casserole

SERVES : 6 - 8   PAN USED : Base & Lid

INGREDIENTS :

½ ounce dried porcini mushrooms

1 cup boiling water

¼ cup plus 1 tablespoon extra virgin olive oil

4 bone in chicken thighs with skin

8 ounces, fresh garlic sausage or unsmoked kielbasa (about 2 links)

Kosher salt and freshly ground pepper

1 medium onion, chopped (about 1 cup)

1 large carrot, cut into 1-inch chunks

2 celery stalks, cut into 1-inch chunks

2 garlic cloves, sliced

2 tablespoons chopped fresh sage

¼ cup tomato paste

1 cup white wine

2 dried bay leaves

3 cups cooked cannellini beans, drained

½ cup fine dry bread crumbs

¼ cup fresh Italian parsley, chopped

PREPARATION :

1. Preheat the oven to 350° F. In a small bowl, soak the porcini in 1 cup boiling water for 15 minutes. Remove the porcini, squeeze dry, and finely chop. Strain and reserve the soaking liquid.

2. In your Dutch oven, heat ¼ cup of the olive oil over medium-high heat. Season the chicken with Kosher salt and freshly ground pepper. Brown the chicken and sausage in 2 batches until well browned all over, about 5 minutes per batch. Remove all of the chicken and sausage to a plate. Add the onions, carrots, and celery and cook until vegetables are lightly caramelized, about 6 minutes. Add the garlic and sage and cook until fragrant, about 1 minute.

3. Make a space in the pan and add the tomato paste and then, cook and stir in that spot until the tomato paste toasts and darkens a shade or two, about 1 to 2 minutes. Stir the tomato paste into the vegetables. Add the wine, bay leaves, and cook until liquid is reduced by half. Add back the chicken and sausage, 3 cups water, and the porcini soaking liquid. Season with Kosher salt and freshly ground pepper. Bring to a simmer, cover, and bake until the chicken is tender, about 45 minutes.

4. Stir in the cannellini beans and just enough water to keep the mixture saucy, about 1 cup. Cover and cook until the chicken and sausage is very tender, about 30 minutes more.

5. Raise the oven temperature to 425° F. In a small bowl, stir together bread crumbs, the remaining 1 tablespoon olive oil, and the chopped parsley. Sprinkle the mixture over the casserole and bake, uncovered, until the crumbs are golden brown, about 10 minutes. Serve hot.

Pro Tip :

Cannellini beans are an excellent choice for casseroles, because they soak up the cooking juices and become extra creamy in texture.

Braised Pork Butt with Cabbage, Sausage, Mustard and Apples

SERVES : 6 - 8   PAN USED : Base & Lid

INGREDIENTS :

Pork roast:

3-4 pound boneless pork shoulder

4 links sweet Italian sausage (about 12 ounces)

3 sprigs rosemary

1 medium spanish onion, sliced

2 braeburn, or other tart apple, peeled, cored sliced thick

1 head green cabbage, sliced

½ pound small white potatoes, cut in half

1 tablespoon caraway seeds

½ cup dijon mustard

2 cups white wine

4 cups chicken stock

White wine vinegar, such as Chardonnay vinegar, to taste

½ cup parsley, chopped

Kosher salt and fresh cracked pepper

Horseradish sauce:

4 tablespoons fresh horseradish, drained

1 cup sour cream

PREPARATION :

1. Fit a wire rack on a sheet tray. Liberally season the pork shoulder with Kosher salt and freshly ground pepper, place on a sheet tray and refrigerate overnight.

2. Heat Dutch oven over medium high heat. Add the sausage to the pan and brown the links on both sides, about 5 minutes per side. Remove the sausage from the pan and reserve on a plate. Fry the sprigs of rosemary in the fat, flipping frequently, about 1 minute or until fragrant. Remove the fried rosemary to a plate and reserve.

3. If the pork shoulder is wet, dry thoroughly with paper towels. Season the pork all over with salt and pepper. Add to Dutch oven and brown on all sides, about 5 minutes per side or until deeply browned. Remove the pork shoulder from the pot to a large plate or baking dish.

4. Add onions, apples, and cabbage to Dutch oven and season with Kosher salt and freshly ground pepper. Cook over medium heat until the vegetables have softened slightly, about 5 minutes. Add the potatoes, caraway, mustard, white wine and cook for another 8 minutes, or until the wine has almost evaporated.

5. Return the pork, sausage and fried rosemary sprigs to the Dutch oven, add the stock, bring to a simmer and cover. Reduce heat to low and braise for at least 3 hours, or until very tender. Season the sauce to taste with white wine vinegar, Kosher salt and freshly ground pepper. Let cool slightly and spoon pork onto plates with a good amount of vegetables and sauce. Serve with horseradish cream.

Pro Tip :

If you want a thicker, richer sauce, strain the broth from the Dutch oven and reduce over medium heat in top pan of Dutch oven until a thin gravy consistency, around 8-10 minutes.

Chatham Cod Pot Roast

SERVES : 4   PAN USED : Base & Lid

INGREDIENTS :

2 Chatham cod filets, skinned, deboned, trimmed and cut into 4-6 ounce portions

1 large butternut or hubbard squash, peeled and cut into large dice

1 medium carrot, peeled and cut into large dice

2 heads of fennel

8 small fingerling potatoes, cooked until tender in salted water

4 shallots, peeled and minced finely

4 large Savoy cabbage leaves, blanched and trimmed of their tough ribs

12 pearl onions, peeled

1 bunch flat leaf Italian parsley, washed and chopped roughly

3 lemons, zested and juiced

4 tablespoons salted butter

1¼ cup white wine

2 cups white fish stock

1 tablespoon honey

2 teaspoons white truffle oil (optional)

Sea salt and freshly ground black pepper

PREPARATION :

1. Arrange the cod filets on a sheet pan. Season generously with salt, pepper, and evenly disperse minced shallots. Top each filet with 1 tablespoon of butter then wrap each filet individually with the savoy cabbage leaves. Refrigerate.

2. Peel the fennel and trim the leaves of their tough fibers with a paring knife. Reserve all peelings and trim for later use. Dice one head of fennel into large squares. Set aside for later use. Roughly cut the remaining fennel and scraps small enough to fit into a juicing machine. Juice all un-diced fennel and reserve for later.

3. In your Dutch oven over low heat combine the carrot, diced fennel, and pearl onions to sweat until translucent. Add in the squash and fingerlings to sweat further until just tender. Deglaze with the wine and reduce by half volume. Add the fish stock and reduce by half. Then, add the fennel juice, reduce for a minute and add in the honey. Carefully arrange the wrapped cod filets in the Dutch oven (the liquid should be about halfway up on the side of the filets) cover with top and transfer to 400°F oven to bake for about 8-10 minutes until cod is just tender.

4. To finish, remove from the oven and transfer to stovetop. Bring the liquid in the Dutch oven to a simmer, making sure to baste the cod filets constantly. Add in the lemon juice and zest, then drizzle the truffle oil all over the fish. Return to simmer to combine flavors, recheck seasoning add in the chopped parsley.

Pro Tip :

Can't find Cod? Haddock or flounder would be a great substitute. Just make sure it's the freshest fish you can find from your fish monger. Paired with a crisp Sauvignon Blanc, you have a perfect meal for a warm summer night on the patio.

Yankee Pot Roast

SERVES : 6 - 8   PAN USED : Base & Lid

INGREDIENTS :

Chuck roast, 3-4 pounds

Kosher salt and freshly ground pepper

3 tablespoon olive oil

2 carrots, cut into 2 inch chunks

3 celery stalks, cut into 2 inch chunks

2 medium onions, cut into 2 inch chunks

6 small turnips, cut in half with stems

3 garlic cloves

3 sprigs fresh thyme

1 sprig fresh rosemary

1 cup carrots, diced

2 dried bay leaves

¼ cup all-purpose flour

½ cup dry red wine

6 cups beef stock

1 pound red potatoes

¼ cup freshly chopped Italian parsley

PREPARATION :

1. Preheat the oven to 350°F. Season the roast with Kosher salt and freshly ground pepper in your Dutch oven over medium-high heat, add the olive oil. When the oil is hot, add the roast and sear on all sides until well browned, about 5 minutes. Remove to a plate.

2. Add the carrots, celery, onions and turnips and saute until caramelized on the edges, about 5 minutes. Add the garlic, thyme, rosemary, bay leaves, and flour. Stir to incorporate the flour into the oil and cook until the flour smells toasty, about 2 minutes.

3. Pour in the wine and bring to a boil. Add the stock and the roast back to the Dutch oven. Bring to a rapid simmer and cover tightly with top. Place in the oven and cook, covered, until the meat is just tender, about 2 hours. Add the potatoes, cover again, and cook until the potatoes are done and the meat is tender (a knife will slide out easily with no resistance), about 30 minutes more. Remove the meat to a cutting board and let the sauce sit for a few minutes and spoon off any fat that has risen to the surface (or pour into a fat-separating measuring cup, pour off the fat, and add the sauce back to the pot).

4. Return the sauce to a simmer and season with Kosher salt and freshly ground pepper, if necessary. Stir in the parsley. Carve the meat into ½ inch thick slices, against the grain, and serve with the sauce and vegetables.

Pro Tip :

When picking your protein for a long roast, look for a chuck, brisket, or round roast for pot roast. They each contain enough connective tissues that will slowly break down into rich collagen, tenderizing the beef and flavoring the gravy as they cook.

Seven Hour Baby Lamb Shoulder

SERVES : 8 - 10   PAN USED : Base & Lid

INGREDIENTS :

3 tablespoons olive oil

4-5 pound baby lamb shoulder

Kosher salt and freshly ground black pepper

2 cups combined carrots, onion and celery, diced

3 tablespoons coriander seeds

2 tablespoons curry powder

½ head of garlic

1 rosemary sprig

3 sprigs thyme

1 quart veal stock

Butchers twine

PREPARATION :

1. Preheat oven to 185°F. In the Dutch oven, heat the oil over medium high heat. Season the lamb shoulder with Kosher salt and freshly ground pepper. Add the lamb and sear it on all sides, about 5 minutes each side. When a nice brown crust has developed all over the meat, remove it from the pan and set it aside on a platter.

2. Lower the heat to medium low and add the celery, onions, carrots, and garlic to the Dutch oven with coriander seeds and curry powder and saute for about 5 minutes, or until the onions are slightly translucent. Meanwhile, make a sachet of herbs by gathering the rosemary and thyme together and tying with butcher's twine.

3. Return the lamb to the Dutch oven and add the stock and the sachet holding the herbs. Bring the liquid to a boil, then cover with the lid of Dutch oven and transfer to the oven. Cook for 7 hours, or until the lamb is tender.

4. Remove the Dutch oven from the oven and remove lid. Let rest for 15 minutes. Transfer the lamb to a cutting board and pull apart with forks. Serve warm with roasted potatoes or vegetables.

Pro Tip :

This is more a technique than a recipe but I wanted to share it with you because this method of cooking results in a superbly moist and tender lamb. The Dutch oven retains the low, slow and even heat necessary to break down the proteins for this cut of meat. If you plan on serving this for Easter, depending on where you live, lamb shoulder may require a special order so be sure to allow time for a butcher to request it.

VEGETABLES

Celery Root Gratin with Gruyere

SERVES : 4 - 6   PAN USED : Base & Lid

INGREDIENTS :

3 cups ½ inch cubes brioche or country bread (4 to 6 slices, depending on the size of the loaf, crust removed)

½ cup extra virgin olive oil

½ cup unsalted butter

1½ teaspoons minced garlic (1 medium clove)

½ teaspoon cayenne pepper

1 dried bay leaf

Small pinch of freshly grated nutmeg

4 medium bulbs celery root, trimmed and sliced thin

2 medium Yukon gold potatoes, peeled and sliced ¼ inch thick

6 cups heavy cream

1 teaspoon Kosher salt

½ teaspoon freshly ground pepper

¼ pound Gruyere cheese, shredded (about 1 cup)

PREPARATION :

1. Preheat the oven to 375°F. Soak the bread cubes in the olive oil.

2. Melt the butter in Dutch oven over medium low heat (do not allow it to color or sizzle). Add the garlic, cayenne, bay leaf and nutmeg. Cook for about 1 minute, then add the celery root and potatoes. Add just enough cream to cover the vegetables. Season with Kosher salt and freshly ground pepper, then bring to a simmer over medium heat and cook until potatoes are nearly tender, about 10 minutes. Drain the potatoes and celery root, discarding the cream and bay leaf.

3. Spoon half the vegetables into lid of Dutch oven. Sprinkle with a bit more than half the cheese. Cover with the remaining celery root and potatoes, followed by the remaining cheese. Top with the remaining oil soaked-bread cubes.

4. Place the top pan of Dutch oven in the oven, uncovered, and bake until the cheese is melted and the gratin is nicely browned on top, 30 to 40 minutes. Serve directly from the oven.

Pro Tip :

A gratin is a great way to magically transform a relatively mundane vegetable into a delicate and luxurious treat. Serve this gratin as an accompaniment to a roasted leg of lamb, pork shoulder, or short ribs.

* Photo on Page 129

Whole Roasted Cauliflower with Cheddar Cheese Sauce

SERVES : 6   PAN USED : Base & Lid

INGREDIENTS :

Cauliflower:

2 teaspoons black peppercorns

8 cloves garlic, smashed with skins on

½ lemon

2 tablespoons olive oil

½ teaspoon garlic powder

1 teaspoon Dijon mustard

½ teaspoon Kosher salt

1 medium head of cauliflower, leaves removed and core cut off to level bottom

Sauce:

2 tablespoons butter

2 tablespoons flour

⅔ cup heavy cream

2½ cups 2% milk

¾ cup white cheddar, shredded

¾ cup fontina cheese, shredded

½ teaspoon Kosher salt

2 teaspoons fresh rosemary, chopped

¼ cup fresh parsley, chopped

Freshly grated nutmeg

PREPARATION :

1. Preheat oven to 450°F. In Dutch oven, bring about 4 quarts of salted water to a boil. Add peppercorns, garlic, and lemon. Lower to a simmer and place cauliflower in, core facing up. Simmer for 15 minutes in poaching liquid or until fork tender. Drain in colander. Place cauliflower right side up in lid of Dutch oven. Whisk with silicone coated whisk olive oil, garlic powder, mustard and salt. Rub all over outside of cauliflower.

2. Place cauliflower in oven and bake for 40-50 minutes until outside is crusty and golden brown.

3. Meanwhile make the cheese sauce. Heat butter in a saucepan on medium to melt. Whisk in flour, and cook for 2 to 3 minutes, stirring constantly, to cook out the starch. Slowly whisk in cream and milk, until smooth. Add salt and bring to a boil, then turn down to simmer. Cook for about 5 minutes, until sauce starts to thicken. Add shredded cheese and whisk, until melted. Cook for one minute, then add rosemary, parsley and a few gratings of fresh nutmeg. Taste, and add a little salt if needed.

4. Once cauliflower is roasted, pour sauce over top and reserve some for dipping.

Pro Tip :

If you want a little extra flavor and char, stick the finished cauliflower with sauce under the broiler until bubbling with char spots.

Baked Beets over Salt with Wedge Salad and Creamy Tarragon Dressing

SERVES : 4   PAN USED : Lid

INGREDIENTS :

8 medium beets, washed but unpeeled

1 pound kosher or coarse sea salt

Extra virgin olive oil

2 tablespoons sour cream

2 tablespoons minced shallots

2 teaspoons tarragon wine vinegar

1½ teaspoons lemon zest

½ teaspoon dijon mustard

Pinch of granulated sugar

¼ cup canola oil

1 tablespoon lemony olive oil

Kosher salt and freshly ground pepper

1 tablespoon fresh tarragon, chopped

1 head crisp iceberg lettuce

PREPARATION :

1. Preheat oven to 375°F. Fill the top pan of Dutch oven with Kosher salt to a depth of about ¼ inch. Place the beets on the salt, evenly spaced, and lightly drizzle with some olive oil. Place in the oven to bake for 30-45 minutes, or until the tip of a sharp knife pierces the beet easily with no resistance.

2. Remove the beets from the oven, and cool. Peel the beets by hand while still warm but easy to handle. Cut them in large chunks, and toss with a generous portion of cracked black pepper.

3. While the beets are roasting, make the dressing. In a small bowl whisk together the sour cream, shallot, vinegar, lemon zest, mustard, and sugar until smooth. Add the canola oil in a stream, whisking, and whisk the vinaigrette until it is emulsified. Whisk in olive oil. Season to taste with Kosher salt and freshly ground pepper.

4. Cut the iceberg lettuce into 4 large wedges. Divide the beets amongst the 4 plates placing beets next to the iceberg wedge. Drizzle lettuce generously with tarragon dressing and chopped tarragon.

Pro Tip :

If you are in a hurry you can microwave the beets. Simply peel and slice them thick, stack them in a microwaveable dish in overlapping pattern, add a little salt, pepper and olive oil and cook on high for 4 to 5 minutes. Then give them the same treatment suggested here, or just add butter.

Spinach Potato Gratin

SERVES : 6 - 8   PAN USED : Base & Lid

INGREDIENTS :

3 tablespoons unsalted butter

2 medium shallots, minced

2 cloves garlic

2 tablespoons fresh sage, chopped

3 cups heavy cream

Pinch of freshly grated nutmeg

3-10 ounce packages frozen spinach, thawed and squeezed dry

2 tablespoons extra virgin olive oil

Kosher salt and freshly ground pepper

2 large yukon gold potatoes

¼ cup freshly grated Parmigiano-Reggiano

1½ cups fresh bread crumbs

2 tablespoons dried oregano

PREPARATION :

1. Melt 2 tablespoons of the butter in the Dutch oven. Add the shallots, garlic and sage, and cook, stirring frequently, until the shallots are translucent, about 2 minutes. Add 2 and ¼ cups of the cream and the nutmeg and bring to a simmer over medium heat. Simmer the cream, stirring occasionally until it is reduced by half, about 20 minutes. Stir in squeezed spinach. Remove from pot into a bowl and set aside.

2. Peel and slice the potatoes into ¼ inch rounds. Place the potato slices into the Dutch oven, add water to cover, and season with 1 teaspoon salt. Bring to a simmer over medium heat, and cook until fork tender but not mushy. Drain the potato slices and place them in a small bowl with the remaining ⅓ cup of cream. Season the potato slices with additional Kosher salt and freshly ground pepper to taste, and gently toss to coat them.

3. Preheat the oven to 375°F. Arrange the potato slices in the lid of Dutch oven. Spread spinach cream mixture evenly over potatoes. Combine bread crumbs with Parmigiano cheese and oregano. Sprinkle evenly over spinach mixture. Bake for 25-30 minutes, or until bubbling and golden brown.

Pro Tip :

Using frozen spinach is a great time saving tip to help get dinner on the table. Frozen fruits and vegetable are picked and preserved at the peak of their freshness, locking in flavor and vitamins.

* Photo on Page 96

Butter Braised Asparagus with Lemon Sauce and Feta

SERVES : 6   PAN USED : Lid

INGREDIENTS :

3 pounds green asparagus, thick

1 to 2 cups chicken stock

3½ tablespoons salted butter

½ teaspoon sea salt, plus more to taste

½ teaspoon freshly ground black pepper, plus more to taste

1 bay leaf, fresh or dried

2 lemons juiced, plus segments (about ¾ cup fresh lemon juice)

2 tablespoons honey

1 cup French feta, crumbled

PREPARATION :

1. Snap off the tough ends of the asparagus spears and peel the stalks with a vegetable peeler or paring knife. Place the spears in Dutch oven. Add enough stock to come about halfway up the sides of the spears. Add 2 tablespoons of the butter, season with the Kosher salt and freshly ground pepper, and place the bay leaf on top. Cover the pan with top pan of Dutch oven, bring to a simmer, and cook over medium heat until the spears are very tender, about 8 minutes.

2. Meanwhile, place the lemon juice and honey in a small non reactive saucepan and simmer over medium heat until reduced by half, about 4 minutes. Whisk in the remaining 1½ tablespoons butter. Season the sauce lightly with Kosher salt and freshly ground pepper and set aside.

3. Drain the asparagus well and arrange equal portions of it on each of six plates. Spoon the lemon segments over the asparagus followed by the crumbled feta. Finish with more freshly ground pepper and Kosher salt.

Pro Tip :

If you can find either Meyer lemon or white asparagus, they both make excellent substitutions in this recipe for regular lemon and green asparagus.

Photo on Page 76

Classic Mac & Cheese

SERVES : 6 - 8   PAN USED : Base & Lid

INGREDIENTS :

1 pound elbow macaroni, cooked
al dente

1½ cups whole milk

½ cup heavy cream

2 teaspoons Worcestershire sauce

¼ cup all-purpose flour

2 teaspoons ground mustard

2 teaspoons garlic powder

¼ teaspoon cayenne pepper

5 tablespoons unsalted butter

8 ounces sharp cheddar, shredded

4 ounces fontina cheese, shredded

Kosher salt and freshly ground pepper

PREPARATION :

1. Preheat the oven to 350°F. Combine milk, heavy cream, and Worcestershire sauce in a small bowl, whisk until smooth.

2. Combine the flour, ground mustard, garlic powder, and cayenne pepper in a small bowl. Place the Dutch oven over medium heat and add the butter. Once butter is melted, add the flour mixture constantly whisking (using a silicone whisk) until smooth. Slowly whisk in the milk mixture until fully combined.

3. Whisk in the cheddar and fontina cheese, reserving ¼ cup of each to top the mac and cheese with. Season with Kosher salt and freshly ground pepper. Add the cooked macaroni to the cheese sauce to coat the macaroni fully.

4. Spoon mac and cheese into lid of Dutch oven. Top with reserved cheese. Place pan on a sheet pan and bake in oven for 20-25 minutes or until cheese on top is melted and golden brown.

Pro Tip :

Outsmart your picky eaters by hiding vegetables in the mac and cheese. Take a mild vegetable, such as carrots, and cook until tender. Puree them with the cream mixture and proceed with the recipe. They'll never know !

Rice and Winter Vegetable Casserole

SERVES : 8   PAN USED : Base & Lid

INGREDIENTS :

Kosher salt

2 cups long grain brown rice

8 tablespoons unsalted butter divided, plus more for the pan

1 pound Brussels sprouts, cut in half through stem

Freshly ground black pepper

4 large eggs

1 cup whole milk

1 cup heavy cream

1 cup scallions, chopped (white and green parts)

½ cup dried cranberries

¼ cup fresh Italian parsley, chopped

1 cup fresh goat cheese, crumbled

½ cup walnuts, chopped

4 tablespoons finely ground bread crumbs

PREPARATION :

1. Preheat the oven to 350°F. In Dutch oven, bring 5 cups of water to a boil with a generous pinch of salt. When the water is boiling, add the rice, reduce to a simmer, cover, and let cook until the rice is just cooked, with still a little chew to it, about 30 to 35 minutes. Remove from the heat, let stand covered, 10 minutes. Fluff with a fork and spread on a sheet pan to dry and let cool.

2. In lid of Dutch oven over medium-high heat, melt 4 tablespoons of the butter. Add the Brussels sprouts cut side down, season with Kosher salt and freshly ground pepper, and let sit in the skillet until browned, about 5 minutes. Stir and cook until the Brussels sprouts are well browned and fork tender. Transfer to a bowl to cool.

3. Lightly butter Dutch oven. In a large bowl, whisk together the eggs, milk, and cream, and then season with salt. Stir in the scallions, parsley, and cranberries. Fold in cool Brussels sprouts and crumbled goat cheese, taking care not to break up the cheese much more. Pour the mixture into the prepared Dutch oven, sprinkle with the bread crumbs and chopped walnuts, and dot the top with the remaining butter pieces. Bake until just set in the center, about 35 to 40 minutes. Let cool for 10 minutes before serving.

Pro Tip :

This would make a great side for your Thanksgiving table. Looking to add a little more color to the dish? Fold in one cup of butternut squash with the Brussels sprouts.

Fluffy Parker House Rolls with Honey Butter and Sea Salt

SERVES : 10   PAN USED : Lid

INGREDIENTS :

Rolls:

¼ cup warm water

½ cup warm milk

¼ cup honey

1⅛ teaspoon yeast

¼ cup (½ stick) butter, softened

¾ teaspoon Kosher salt

2½ cups flour

1 egg, whisked until combined for egg wash

Honey butter:

¼ cup salted butter, room temperature

2 tablespoons honey

Sea salt for sprinkling

PREPARATION :

To make the rolls:

1. Combine the warm water, milk, and yeast and set aside for about 10 minutes or until the yeast is active and bubbling.

2. In a stand mixer with a dough hook, combine the yeast mixture, honey, butter, salt, and flour. Mix and knead, adding more flour if necessary, until the dough leaves the sides of the bowl and clings to the dough hook, about 8 minutes.

3. Transfer the dough to a floured surface and knead a few times. Divide dough into 10 balls, pinching the seams on the underside to make a smooth top. Place formed rolls into the lid of your Dutch oven, leaving space between each one. Let the rolls rise in a warm place for 2 hours, until doubled in size. Brush with egg wash. Bake for about 20 minutes at 350°F.

To make the butter:

1. While rolls are baking make honey butter. In stand mixer or small bowl whisk softened butter until smooth, then add honey. Whip on medium speed for one minute until very creamy. Serve warm rolls with honey butter and sea salt.

Pro Tip :

Make sure to check expiration dates on your yeast before starting any baking project. It is crucial in providing the soft, pillowy texture we all love in these rolls.

Butternut Squash Risotto

SERVES : 4 - 6   PAN USED : Base

INGREDIENTS :

Roasted butternut squash:

1 cinnamon stick

1 whole clove

1 teaspoon freshly ground nutmeg

4 allspice berries

4 tablespoons clarified butter

1 small butternut squash, halved
and deseeded

Risotto:

½ large onion, diced

½ cup white wine

4 cups chicken or vegetable stock

1½ cups risotto or Arborio rice

2 oranges, zested

3 tablespoons fresh sage, chopped

3 tablespoons unsalted butter

½ cup Parmesan cheese, grated

Toasted pine nuts

PREPARATION :

1. Preheat oven to 375°F. Grind cinnamon sticks, clove, nutmeg and all spice in spice grinder. Cut butternut squash in half. Brush inside with clarified butter and dust each one with the spice mixture. Place in Dutch oven and roast until tender, about 45-60 minutes. Remove from oven and when cool enough to handle scoop out into a bowl.

2. Place Dutch oven over low heat, add onions and sweat until translucent. Add in risotto and stir. Add wine and reduce until almost dry (stirring constantly). Next add 3½ cups stock and butternut squash meat and cook for about 5 minutes. Add in orange zest and cook for 2 more minutes, stirring constantly. Test that it is al dente, adding more stock if needed. Finish with sage, butter, cheese, Kosher salt and freshly ground pepper to taste. Top with toasted pine nuts and serve.

Pro Tip :

When it is peak squash season in the fall, substitute mini pumpkins for the butternut squash. Bake until tender, and scoop out the flesh and proceed with the recipe. Use the hollowed out pumpkins to serve the risotto in, adding a festive and fun touch to your table.

Roasted Tomatoes with Provencal Bread Crumb Crust

SERVES : 6   PAN USED : Lid

INGREDIENTS :

Kosher salt

2 pounds tomatoes, sliced thick

¼ cup extra -virgin olive oil, plus more for drizzling

Freshly ground black pepper

2 cups unseasoned fresh bread crumbs

2 small shallots, finely chopped

½ cup fresh basil, chopped

½ cup fresh Italian parsley, chopped

½ cup scallions, chopped, (white and green parts)

2 garlic cloves, finely chopped

¼ cup Parmigiano-Reggiano, freshly grated

PREPARATION :

1. Preheat the oven to 375°F. Arrange sliced tomatoes in lid of Dutch oven. Season with Kosher salt and freshly ground pepper.

2. In large bowl, combine the bread crumbs, shallots, basil, parsley, scallions, and garlic. Season with Kosher salt and freshly ground pepper. Drizzle with the oil and toss well with a fork to combine.

3. Sprinkle the crumb mixture over the tomatoes so that the tomatoes are almost completely obscured by the crumbs. Sprinkle with the cheese and drizzle with a bit more oil. Roast until the edges of the tomatoes are browned and the crumbs are crisp and golden, 20-25 minutes. Serve family style while still hot.

Pro Tip :

This simple cooking method highlights the cast iron properties. The high heat of roasting cooks the vegetables quickly, and doing so, retains their moisture. Apply this technique to whatever is in season, blanching the vegetables first in salted water if they are on the crisper side.

Photo on Page 129

Friendsgiving Sweet Potato Casserole

SERVES : 4   PAN USED : Base & Lid

INGREDIENTS :

2 pounds sweet potatoes, peeled and sliced thick

8 tablespoons unsalted butter

1 vanilla bean, split

2 allspice berries

1 cinnamon stick

1 banana

1 piece star anise

1 orange, quartered

3 tablespoons maple syrup

½ cup heavy cream

Kosher salt and freshly ground pepper

3 cups mini marshmallows

PREPARATION :

1. Fill your Dutch oven with salted water and cook the sweet potatoes in boiling water until very soft, about 20 minutes. Drain the potatoes, then cover and keep warm.

2. Meanwhile, melt 2 tablespoons of the butter in Dutch oven. Add the vanilla bean, allspice, cinnamon, and star anise. Toast the spices, stirring occasionally, until they are fragrant, about 3 minutes. Add the orange quarters and banana slices, raise the heat to medium high, and cook, turning the ingredients regularly, until they brown slightly, about 2 minutes per side. Add the maple syrup to the pan, lower the heat, and simmer for a few minutes. Remove from heat and set aside to allow the flavors to meld for about 30 minutes.

3. Squeeze the juice from the orange quarters into the syrup mixture, and discard the peels. Remove and discard the spices carefully, making sure not to lose any of the syrup. Puree the cooked sweet potatoes in a food processor, slowly adding the cream and the remaining 6 tablespoons of butter. Add the banana mixture and puree until fully incorporated. Season to taste with Kosher salt and freshly ground pepper.

4. Spread the sweet potato puree in the lid of the Dutch oven. Sprinkle with the mini marshmallows and cook until marshmallow are golden brown and melted, about 20 minutes.

Pro Tip :

Wouldn't this make a fantastic side dish for your Friendsgiving table? It pairs really well with turkey and can be prepped up to 2 days in advance. Just refrigerate after placing sweet potato mixture in pan. The day of, top with marshmallow and cook until toasty and heated through, about 30 minutes.

Photo on Page 128

02

03

SWEETS

Cast Iron Apple Tart Tatin

SERVES : 6 - 8   PAN USED : Lid

INGREDIENTS :

One 14-ounce package all-butter puff pastry

6 tablespoons unsalted butter

⅔ cup sugar

7 Braeburn apples, or other firm tart apples peeled, cored, and halved lengthwise

Vanilla ice cream

PREPARATION :

1. On a lightly floured work surface, roll out the puff pastry 1/8 inch thick. Take the top of your Dutch oven and use it to trace an oval about one inch larger than the lid. Transfer to a baking sheet and refrigerate; reserve the pastry scraps for another use.

2. In the lid of your Dutch oven, melt the butter. Add the sugar and cook over moderately low heat, stirring occasionally, until the sugar is dissolved and the mixture comes to a simmer, about 2 minutes. Remove from the heat. Arrange the apple halves core side down in the lid in 2 snug concentric circles. Return to the heat and cook on medium low, undisturbed until a light amber caramel forms, about 15-20 minutes.

3. Preheat the oven to 375°F. Top the apples with the puff pastry, tucking in around the edges and bake on a sheet pan lined with parchment for about 30-40 minutes (or until the pastry is golden brown delicious, the caramel is deep amber colored and the apples are tender). Let cool for 15 minutes.

4. Place a large oval plate on top of the skillet and carefully invert the tart. Serve warm with crème fraîche.

Pro Tip :

Without the non-stick coating, it would be very difficult to make this dish in a cast iron pan. However, with the non-stick, this Tart Tatin is as easy as pie. Pears or quince would be a delicious substitute for the apples, or use a combination of your favorite fall fruits.

Blueberry Ginger Oat Crisp

SERVES : 6 - 8   PAN USED : Lid

INGREDIENTS :

4 cups blueberries, fresh or frozen

½ cup granulated sugar

2 tablespoons cornstarch

1 teaspoon grated fresh ginger

Finely grated zest and juice of 1 lemon

½ cup all-purpose flour

½ cup light brown sugar (packed)

½ cup rolled oats

½ teaspoon ground cinnamon

Pinch of Kosher salt

6 tablespoons cold, unsalted butter, cut into pieces

Lightly sweetened whipped cream, for serving

2 tablespoons candied ginger, coarsely chopped

PREPARATION :

1. Preheat the oven to 350°F. In a medium bowl, toss the berries with the sugar, cornstarch, grated ginger, lemon zest and juice. Let sit at room temperature 15 minutes, stirring occasionally.

2. For the topping, in a food processor, add the flour, brown sugar, cinnamon, and salt and pulse to combine. Add the oats and sprinkle with the butter pieces on top. Pulse in quick bursts just until the butter is distributed and the size of peas.

3. Pour berry mixture into lid of Dutch oven and place on baking sheet lined with parchment. Using a spoon, spread berries evenly in pan. Sprinkle the topping evenly over all of the top of the fruit, do not pack down. It may seem like a lot of topping, but use it all, as it sinks into the crumbles as they bake. Bake until the topping is crisp and brown and the berries are bubbling, about 45 minutes. Let cool 10 minutes before serving, but the crumbles are best served warm, with a dollop of whipped cream and a sprinkle of the candied ginger.

Pro Tip :

Brown sugar is an essential ingredient in a crisp. Ever reach into your pantry to find either hard brown sugar or *gasp*, no brown sugar? You can revive it once by microwaving the sugar in a bowl covered with a wet paper towel for about 20-25 seconds, or you can make your own. Simply mix 1-2 tablespoons molasses into 1 cup granulated sugar with your hands in a small bowl until evenly distributed. You get to control the intensity of the molasses flavor and you'll never run out again.

Balsamic Roasted Strawberries

SERVES : 6 - 8   PAN USED : Base & Lid

INGREDIENTS :

2 pints of strawberries, hulled and cut in half

¼ cup brown sugar

½ teaspoon vanilla extract

1 cup balsamic vinegar

PREPARATION :

1. Preheat the oven to 400°F.

2. Whisk together the balsamic vinegar, brown sugar and vanilla in a bowl. In another bowl, pour 1/4 of the liquid on the strawberries and toss to coat. Spread into top pan of Dutch oven and roast for 12 minutes.

3. Meanwhile, transfer remaining liquid into Dutch oven and set over high heat. Once it reaches a boil, cook until liquid has reduced in half and is a syrupy consistency, this will happen quickly.

4. Remove strawberries from the oven and pour balsamic reduction over strawberries and toss to coat.

Pro Tip :

These strawberries would be equally good for breakfast over thick greek yogurt, as well as a topping for ice cream. My personal favorite is olive oil ice cream with this compote, adding a little cracked black pepper for contrast.

Saffron Poached Pears

SERVES : 4   PAN USED : Base

INGREDIENTS :

8 Seckel pears (or 4 small Bartlett pears), peeled, cut in half, and cored

2 cups sugar

2 cups white wine

1 vanilla bean, split and scraped, seeds discarded

4 cardamom pods, crushed

1 piece star anise

1 cinnamon stick

½ lemon

Pinch of saffron threads

Sour cream, for serving

PREPARATION :

1. Combine the sugar, vanilla bean, star anise, cinnamon, lemon and saffron threads in Dutch oven. Add 2 cups of water and the white wine to the sugar mixture and bring to a boil over medium-high heat. Add the pears. Reduce the heat to low and cook gently for 25-30 minutes. Allow to cool a bit in the syrup.

2. While still warm, place 2 pear halves (or 1 if using Bartlett) in a bowl, ladling some poaching liquid around them. Add a spoonful of sour cream next to the pears and serve.

Pro Tip :

The smell in your house will be intoxicating after adding cinnamon and the other spices to the saffron poaching liquid. When preparing the poaching liquid, if you are unsure how to split and scrape a fresh vanilla bean pod, google it and watch a quick video. The finished pears can be served with sour cream as suggested or alongside a wedge of cheesecake for something more substantial.

Skillet S'mores Dip

SERVES : 6 - 8   PAN USED : Lid

INGREDIENTS :

1 10 ounce bag semi-sweet chocolate chips

1 10 ounce bag marshmallows (mini or regular)

2 tablespoon butter

Graham crackers

PREPARATION :

1. Preheat the oven to 425°F. Melt butter in the lid of the Dutch oven on medium low heat and then add the chocolate chips to completely cover the bottom of the pan, stirring until smooth and melted.

2. Add marshmallows to completely cover the chocolate. Bake in the oven on the middle rack for 15-20 minutes.

3. Once the marshmallows are golden brown take the pan out of the oven and let cool for 5 minutes. Use the graham crackers for dipping and enjoy.

Pro Tip :

If you like your marshmallows to have a campfire look, move the skillet to the top rack for 1-2 minutes and turn on the broiler. Watch them closely because they will char quickly!

Dulce De Leche

SERVES : 6 - 8   PAN USED : Base & Lid

INGREDIENTS :

4 cans sweetened condensed milk
14-16 ounce

1 vanilla bean split and scraped,
seeds and pod reserved

A few pinches salt

4 pint sized canning jars with a
clean two-piece lid

PREPARATION :

1. Divide vanilla amongst the 4 clean pint caning jars. Open the cans of sweetened condensed milk and pour it into the jars, scraping the cans to be sure to get all of the sweetened condensed milk. Add a pinch of salt to each jar. Screw the lid in place to fingertip tightness, then slowly invert and turn the jar right-side-up several times to distribute ingredients.

2. Put the jars in the Dutch oven base and add hot tap water to it to cover the jars by an inch. Cover the lid and set the heat to low and let it cook for 8 to 12 hours, replenishing water occasionally to keep above the jars. When the cooking time is up, remove from heat, remove the lid, and let it stand undisturbed until the water reaches room temperature. Rinse the jars, refrigerate, and use within 2 weeks.

Pro Tip :

What wouldn't you want to eat this on? Dulce de leche makes a delicious dip for apple slices, a filler between cake layers, on ice cream or just straight up on a spoon in front of the refrigerator.

Sweet and Salty Nutty Chocolate Bark

SERVES : 6 - 8 (makes about 24 pieces)   PAN USED : Base & Lid

---

INGREDIENTS :

1½ tablespoons unsalted butter

¾ cup sugar

2 cups roasted whole mixed nuts

1½ bittersweet chocolate chips

Sea salt for sprinkling

PREPARATION :

1. Line a baking sheet with either parchment paper or a silicone baking mat. Add sugar to the lid of the Dutch oven. Place over low heat and cook without stirring but swirling the pan, caramelize until medium golden brown, about the color of an old penny. Remove from heat and whisk in butter. Add nuts all at once to pan and stir to coat evenly with the caramel. Pour the nuts onto the lined baking sheet, spreading evenly to distribute without clumps. Let cool and then break into clumps. Wash out lid

2. Bring about 1 inch of water to a simmer in base of Dutch oven. Invert lid onto base, creating a double boiler, and add chocolate. When the chocolate is about two-thirds melted, remove from double boiler and continue to stir until completely melted. Add cooled nuts and spread on the same baking sheet in a thin uniform layer. Let stand for 5 minutes and then sprinkle lightly with sea salt.

3. Chill in the refrigerator until firm, at least 2 hours, and then break into 1 or 2 inch pieces. Store in a cool, dry place, stacked between layers of parchment paper in an airtight container. The bark will keep, tightly wrapped for up to two weeks.

Pro Tip :

Other than having a piece alongside a double espresso, one of my favorite uses for this bark is to chop up and sprinkle over black raspberry ice cream.

About the Author

Geoffrey Zakarian is chef/partner at The Lambs Club and The National in New York City, Point Royal and Counter Point in Hollywood, Florida and oversees the food and beverage hospitality at The Water Club at Borgata in New Jersey. He is a judge on Food Network's Chopped, is an Iron Chef on Iron Chef America and is a cohost of the Emmy-nominated weekend talk show, The Kitchen. Outside of television and his restaurant kitchens, Chef Zakarian has developed a line of gourmet essentials and culinary tools, including the revolutionary Zakarian Non-Stick Cast Iron cookware. Zakarain resides in New York City and serves as chairman of City Harvest's Food Council.

To learn more about Chef Zakarian, his restaurants, and products, visit geoffreyzakarian.com

A Note of Thanks

I would like to take a moment to thank all of those who helped this cookbook come to life. It takes tremendous effort and many hands to test, taste, photograph, edit and tell a story through a book filled with delicious recipes. Most certainly, I could not do all of this alone, and I sincerely appreciate all of the support and passion that the individuals in the following list dedicated to bringing these pages to your home kitchen:

Anthony Candella and Margaret Zakarian, creative directors; Eric Haugen and Luci Levere, contributing chefs; KC and Gail Kratt, kc Kratt photography; Jill Gedra, Edward Forester, Kusé, Kim Villanueva, Evan & Rachel Dash, Jenna Lonergan, Shelby Scott, Cat Reinhard, Sarah Spring and the entire Storebound and Zakarian teams.

Recipe Index

Recipe Index

Recipe Index

Recipe Index